D0530469

TRUST YATES!

TRUST YATES!

Stories of a guide dog with a dog collar

Mike Endicott

Terra Nova Publications

First published by Terra Nova Publications Ltd, 2000
Reprinted 2001

All rights reserved.

© Mike Endicott 2000

Mike Endicott asserts the moral right
to be identified as the author of this work.

No part of this publication may be reproduced or
transmitted in any form or by any means, electronic
or mechanical, including photocopy, recording or any
information storage and retrieval system, without
permission in writing from the publisher.

Published in Great Britain by
Terra Nova Publications Ltd
PO Box 2400
Bradford on Avon, Wiltshire BA15 2YN

Scripture quotations taken from the
Holy Bible, New International Version. Copyright
© 1973, 1978, 1984 by International Bible Society.
Used by permission of Hodder and Stoughton Ltd.
All rights reserved.

ISBN 1-9019-4908-7

Cover design: Gazelle Creative Productions
Line drawings by Amanda Endicott

Printed in Great Britain at
The Cromwell Press, Trowbridge, Wiltshire

Contents

Foreword

I first heard of Mike Endicott when my son, David, fell off a mosque (don't ask!) in Turkey, and broke his pelvis in three places. Because of the incredibly swirling complications that followed this accident I was unable to get to a speaking engagement in Gloucestershire, and Mike very kindly took my place.

He turned a failed evening into a highly enjoyable experience for all those who were there. It was great for me as well, because, as an indirect result, I had a chance to read this book in manuscript form. I get to read a lot of books in manuscript form and I can tell you that the experience is not always a pleasant or edifying one. This time it was pure pleasure. I challenge you, as you read this book, not to fall in love with Yates, his owner and the master that Mike serves. Jesus was a superb storyteller, and the tradition is carried on by this writer. With warmth, wit and wisdom he uses a succession of charming tales to seamlessly educate and re-educate us in the endless revelation of God's love. The laughter and lessons of the chapter entitled 'Crumbs' will stay with me for a very long time.

It was a real joy for me to spend time with Mike and his wonderful dog. I am confident that it will be an equally joyful experience for you.

Adrian Plass

Introduction

As with every guide dog, Yates was carefully chosen for me. His own personality and lifestyle had to be as good a match as possible to my own. Even the choice of colour was deliberate. The Guide Dogs for the Blind Association (GDBA) thought that a black coat with a white harness might make for suitable colour co-ordination with the habitual dress of an Anglican clergyman! His name, Yates, seemed quite unusual. I had expected a Sally or a Patch, but not a Yates. His mother is a golden retriever and his father a black Labrador, both of them kept by the GDBA especially for breeding. As each litter is born, the Association selects a letter of the alphabet and then chooses the puppies' names. This time the letter was 'Y' and the litter was eleven—naming that lot must have been quite a challenge!

Guide dogs have been training for almost two years by the time the would-be owner gets to meet them. In that time they learn social skills, obedience and then guiding—a massive amount of instruction. Up to four weeks of intense training for the owner then takes place before owner and dog are allowed out into the world on their own.

Yates' mixed parenting has resulted in a black Labrador with a slightly longer nose than is usual in the breed, and longer legs that give him just the right height to suit me. I would love to think of him as being as much a retriever as a Labrador, but I cannot. He does not retrieve. He is a great one for charging flat out around the garden and is eager to chase after any missile hurled over his head. But retrieve it? He does manage to return with the object about half way only; perhaps that is because he is only half a retriever!

At the other end of his black and shiny body is a tail. This never stops moving. It can be very welcome and cooling on hot summer days, but can also add annoyingly to the draught in icy winter churches.

At first I had supposed, because of the tail, that he had ambitions to be a helicopter when he grew up, because of the incessant practice going on at the rear end. But since then he has sometimes looked with wistful jealousy at Shetland ponies. Perhaps his longings lie elsewhere.

One thing is for sure: he is very beautiful. I cannot say that is true from my own observations, but from the never ceasing adoration he receives, mostly from ladies in the street! At first I found this most perturbing. Standing at pelican crossings, waiting for the bleeper to signal, seems to Yates to be a wonderful place to pose. We can almost guarantee that some kind lady will approach, saying: "Aren't you just gorgeous!" They will be talking to the dog, naturally.

The strangest thing of all is that Yates is three dogs in one. Let loose in a field, he behaves as one would expect: running, cavorting, sniffing, and anything else normal dogs do in fields. My putting his lead around his neck changes him immediately into a second dog. He becomes the best trained house pet I have ever come across. Walking to heel, sitting, waiting, lying down—every command is obediently acted upon. When he dresses in his working gear—his harness—he changes again, dramatically. He is in control, the boss, the responsible one. No laughing or giggling now; no unnecessary movement; no lack of control. He is responsible for what is happening to us, and he is only too well aware of it. Now decisions have to be made. Now he has to watch everything. There are gaps, gateways, pavement kerbs and passing cars. Children who dive towards him must not ruffle even one feather. What about the height of that sign—is there room for Dad underneath? What about those two ladies coming out of that shop backwards? They are lost in conversation about surgical operations: will they notice us? Then there are bollards, street furniture of all kinds, lamp posts to be avoided, gaps between passers-by to be measured. Worst of all are the children sitting on the benches outside McDonalds, beefburger and chips in hand. Now he must really keep calm! Life on the open road is action packed for him. He makes decisions by the hundred, every inch of the way, and every one with the cool head of a dog who knows exactly what he is doing.

Our first real outing beyond the local shops was to minister at a residential retreat in a healing centre in England. At the end of the final service, one of the guests came up to me and said, "I've come to say goodbye. Thank you for all your hard work. Actually, I learned more about my relationship with God, and what it should be, by watching you go about the place with Yates!" Coming home after that week, I began to ponder on what she might have seen, and started to keep a record of short tales of Yates and the things that I was learning from them. By the time I put them all together, Yates and I had been a partnership for two and a half years. We have grown to be inseparable. In that short time there have been many hilarious occasions and some more thought provoking ones, each one a little story in itself.

Of course, Yates does not actually converse in English with me—the words I credit him with in this book are only in my imagination. Being without sight means that I miss most of his body language, too. I have had to rely on the comments of others to fill in the picture. Nevertheless, he has taught me a great deal.

1

Getting Started

Then God said, "Let us make man in our image, in our likeness, and let them rule over the fish of the sea and the birds of the air, over the livestock, over all the earth, and over all the creatures that move along the ground."

Genesis 1:26

The decision had been made, the forms signed; the long summer of waiting was over. It was my sister who had persuaded me in the end. She had been the proud owner of three guide dogs by then, and could not speak highly enough of the advantages.

Deciding to have a guide dog is not the same as inviting a pet into the home; it is much more like a husband and wife trying to decide to have children. The discussion goes back and forth; the details are all gone into. The pros and cons are weighed and measured, the advantages and disadvantages balanced. But, in the end, the final decision is not at all rational. It is much more like saying, "Oh heck, let's just go for it!"

So here I was, feeling bewildered and insecure, in the guide dog training school.

Two days into the course, and Yates sat in the middle of my bedroom floor at the guide dog training centre, eyeing me up and down with nervous interest. For my part, I sat on the edge of the bed, wondering how a mere human begins a relationship with a dog. He felt uncomfortable in a strange place with a stranger, and I felt helpless. What a way to start!

He sat and looked at me, and I sat and stared back, without either of us having the slightest idea what was going on in the mind of the other. 'He is big,' I remember thinking, 'nearly two years old now, and too big to argue with!'

On that first evening of our relationship, I did not know one single doggy command with which to approach him and start a conversation. He did not look as if he was about to make friends too easily, either. How was this thing going to work? Were we about to spend four weeks just looking at each other in the September sunshine?

Even after all the lectures about how wonderfully trained guide dogs are, how carefully bred and selected, how gentle and perfectly faithful, he was still a big black dog I had never come across before, and there he was, right in front of me— measuring.

Who was going to be the boss? This would be the first question, and both of us knew that our relationship was not going anywhere until we had got that one sorted out. Feeling that the first move was probably up to me, I patted my knee encouragingly and called to him, "Come on, Yates!" There was a lengthy gap to allow a considered opinion to form in his mind, and I tried again: "Come on, Yates!"

The black heap on the floor sighed noisily, stood up, and turned around to face the other way, pointedly presented me with his backside and lay down on the floor again. His reaction said it all. Battle had been joined.

Leaving him alone in the room for a few minutes, I returned to find him quite at home, sprawled out like a dining Roman along the length of my bed. This I later understood to be an important move on his part. Laying claim to, and taking over, the nest of a rival in the pack is all part of establishing social hierarchy. If I had let him stay there, he would have won the first round with flying colours! "Get off!" I yelled at him in the most 'parade ground' and intentionally frightening tone I could muster, and he slunk onto the floor in disgrace. The relief in me positively sighed. Round two to me!

In the days and weeks that followed at the training centre, there were to be many more such battles—some large and obvious; some small and subtle. Each time, I felt like giving up, not being a 'tussler' by nature. But this was a course that one could either pass or fail. Success would mean stepping out into a sighted world with a mere animal as a navigator, and failure would mean—what? More of the same as before. Failure here would mean, for the foreseeable future, going on with the frustration of having to rely on others all the time, just to get me down the street, let alone to have any independence worth having. Then there would be all the commands to learn: hundreds of them, it seemed at the time.

Walking out with Yates in his harness brought back all my teenage memories of learning to drive. Panic! Did I do this right? Did I do that wrong? Is this safe? How can I possibly remember all the right moves?

There was a story being told around that time about a concert the famous pianist, Paderewski, was about to hold. Apparently, an air of expectancy filled the crowded hall as the audience anxiously awaited the entrance of the maestro. A nine year old boy, impatient with waiting and fascinated by the magnificent Steinway grand piano on centre stage, slipped away unnoticed from his parents and made his way up through the flowers and onto the platform. After examining the beautiful instrument in great detail for a few moments, blissfully oblivious to the nearby presence of the packed audience, the boy sat down on the piano stool and began to play a rendition of his most polished party-piece, 'Chopsticks'.

There must have been a deathly hush as the audience sucked half the air in the hall in through their teeth. Some began to snigger. Another called out in anger, "Whose child is that?" followed by the not too kind question, "Can't somebody do something about this?"

From behind the wings, Paderewski looked out to see what

all the fuss was about. Quickly summing up the situation, he quietly slipped onto the stage behind the boy and, reaching over him, began to play a beautiful counter-harmony around the child's melody. "Keep playing," Paderewski whispered to the boy. "Don't stop. Play on. You're doing magnificently. Just don't quit!"

And that's exactly what Jesus does for each one of us when we surrender our heart and life to him. He comes beside us, no matter what our situation, and whispers, "Don't stop. Keep playing. Don't give up. I'm here beside you to help you; to encourage you; to enrich your life. Just don't quit. Trust me, and I will make something beautiful out of all this."

So I did not quit, fumbling on through the course, getting some things right and some terribly wrong, but we made it— we got there! And somewhere in those first four weeks at the training centre, Yates and I became friends for life.

2

Platform of trust

Those who trust in the LORD are like Mount Zion, which cannot be shaken but endures forever. As the mountains surround Jerusalem, so the LORD surrounds his people both now and for evermore.

Psalm 125:1

One of the first things that God requires of us when we become Christians is that we begin to learn to trust him. Many new Christians find themselves in places of trial that have been allowed by God so that they may turn tighter towards him.

The same thing is true of guide dog training. As soon as it is deemed to be safe enough, the unsuspecting guide dog owner is placed in situations where he has to learn to start trusting.

I have a clear memory of being bundled into a van, and being dropped back out of it right at the opposite end of the crowded local shopping centre. "Find your own way back!" they told us, with expectation a great deal higher than our faith.

Two things then happened to make it all very easy: one seen and one unseen. To my surprise, I found it easy to ask for directions. I discovered that I could actually stop people in the street and ask the way. What a relief to be able to do that! Yates' white harness is a telling badge: no need for explanations any more, and no need for embarrassment at missing signals or body language.

Before the days of Yates, it was easy to scare people, putting them off their guard by rushing up and asking for directions to a shop which was only a few feet away. This was going to be a lot easier than I thought.

The other—yet unseen—help was there all the time, in the form of the instructors. We thought we had been deserted, but they were there constantly. Keeping their distance, they walked behind each of us, in contact with one another over hand-held radios. But, then, it is not difficult to keep out of sight when working with blind people!

Just as we left the crowded town shopping centre, full of self-satisfaction, we came to the park. It would all be downhill, now. The worst was over. The shopping centre battlefield was conquered. Now we could take it easy and just roll on home. Yates set off at a good pace, knowing the route we had to take. For two or three hundred yards we bravely strode across the park. Suddenly, there it was. I could hear the ducks quacking and splashing on the river. Sheer fear rose up from somewhere deep in my guts, setting my teeth on edge. What will he do now? What usually happens when a dog sees a flock of ducks playing in the water? Was I about to finish up waist-deep in the river? I could not let go of him. That would be no solution: letting go of a guide dog simply puts the brakes on—he stands firm where he is, unmoving, until the handle is lifted again. Then what? Back to the ducks?

Did I really trust him? If I was unsure of Yates, would I trust God? The verse of an old song that my wife Ginnie used to sing floated across my mind:

> *I leaned my back against an oak,*
> *Thinking it was a trusty tree.*
> *But first it bent and then it broke,*
> *Just as my love proved false to me.*

Most human beings have experienced that sort of betrayal once too often. Friends break faith with us. We find out that they have been busy behind our backs, while being charming to our faces. Families may evaporate at our times of greatest need. At such moments, it can seem as though love and God let us down.

What we need at these times—and I needed him now—is the God who holds us far safer than even the best of parents could ever do; the One who is steadfastly there for us: who does not mind how much our noses run when we weep.

Yates is a king among dogs. He marched purposefully along the riverside path, offering the ducks a sideways glance of interest only. On he strode, neither flinching nor inching off his determined path. Worry is such a real and human thing, but what a waste of spiritual energy it so often turns out to be! What a lesson it was to learn at first hand that we can trust in the presence of the Master.

However, once was not enough for the instructors. More pain was at hand. Bundled back into the van, we found ourselves deposited at the local railway station. On to the platform, down the underpass, along under the tracks and up the other side. So far so good. As if it had been planned this way, a train was waiting. "Find the door!" I commanded, according to instruction. Yates did not hesitate: he walked purposefully and directly to the first available carriage door, and on to the train we clambered.

The next command quickly followed: "Find a seat!" He found a suitable one, placing his nose on it to indicate to me its position. We had to hurry because the train would soon be setting off. Back we went to the door, jumping down on to the platform. "How do I know to get out the right side?" I tentatively asked, aware that there would not always be a crowd to follow off the train. Getting through an open door on the opposite side to the platform could result in a nasty fall.

"That's easy," came the reply. "Open the door and tell your dog to go forwards. If the lead disappears out of your hand you've opened the wrong door!"

Before I knew it, I was in trouble again. The train had gone now, leaving a gaping hole in front of me.

"Just move your right foot slightly forward, and tell me what you feel," asked the instructor.

Yates had stopped for something—I had no idea what. It could have been a narrow gap, or a pile of suitcases. I was hoping it was anything other than what it was. My right toe inched forward into space. Mustering up my bravest face, I told the instructor: "My guess is that this is the edge of the platform."

"Yup, you've got it!"

'Well,' I told myself, 'that was an easy test.' I guessed the answer correctly, and I can go home now. But it wasn't over.

"Now tell the dog to go forwards." She had to be joking! By now, I had begun to understand the depth of the obedience training that Yates had received. If I told him to go forward, then he would.

The instructor continued: "What's in front of you?" she asked again.

"About a three foot drop to lots of heavy gravel and a load of iron bars on railway sleepers," I offered, sheepishly.

"Then tell the dog to go forwards," she repeated.

There were some options here. I could refuse. That would be sensible. I could give the order, and then let go. That would be practical. I could just run away in fear. That would be human. Then a lower, softer, voice came alongside my other ear:

"Learn to trust, whatever happens."

"Forward!" I ordered, in my best and firmest voice. Yates stood up. If it were going to happen, it would happen now. He stepped delicately across my feet, so that he stood along the very edge of the platform, leaned his great shoulders into my knees and pushed. He pushed hard, forcing me to take a step backwards to steady myself. Then he coolly stepped to the right, pulling around to face the opposite way and took two strides forwards, to put distance between me and potential danger.

"That's my dog," I smiled to myself.

3

Sparkling

Surely God does not reject a blameless man or strengthen the hands of evildoers. He will yet fill your mouth with laughter and your lips with shouts of joy.

Job 8:20

The first winter Yates and I were together, we took a train down to south-west Wales. He spent most of the journey sucking a discarded banana skin that he found under the seat. Unhappily, railway timetables have never been tuned to coincide with church services, so we arrived too early and had to sit for half an hour in the church before the service was due to begin. It was a well designed building, I remember. It had a wood block floor, and chairs instead of the ancient wooden pews that we too often have to put up with in our churches. The sanctuary was screened off, and all the chairs had been turned around to face a stage at the back, where a Sunday School nativity play was due to take place a few days later.

Yates, ever patient, settled in to wait. He stretched out on one side and slept for a while, then turned over to get more comfortable on his other flank. Just before the service was about to start, his major blessing of the evening arrived, in the form of a twelve year old girl, obviously a dog lover. As she bent over him, he rolled on his back to allow her better access.

"Come on, friend, get going on the old chest!" She duly obliged, scratching and hugging him to his heart's delight. The service started and the singing began. Then we got the nod. Saddled up and ready to go, Yates took me up into the sanctuary, with all its bright lights. We turned to face the congregation, my mind racing in its last-minute way through the major points I wanted to make. I had no chance. As we turned to face the congregation, there was a murmur, and then a giggle, which rose and swelled into full-scale laughter. I was mortified. What had happened? Why all the amusement? What on earth was going on? I wanted to quieten them down: I had some really important things to say. The great moment in which such godly wisdom was about to pour from my lips was lost to me. How would I ever get the people back in the mood? By now they were all in full hysterics, and I was overcome by the strangest feeling that most of the angels in heaven were rocking too. What's more, now I was grinning with them. Our capacity for having fun is part of our created make-up, and therefore, presumably, comes from God.

I began wondering whether or not God is amused by my sermons, and how he would find the one I was about to give. When we struggle with some theological nicety, perhaps beginning to perplex our listeners, and maybe even to confuse ourselves, it's easy to imagine God waiting to suggest the thought, "You're confusing them! Just stop a moment, and tell them that I love them." Sometimes, thankfully rarely nowadays, on these preaching visits with Yates, there arrives that dreaded moment when I seem to lose my train of thought in the middle of a talk. Perhaps God is not displeased when this happens— especially if the lecture isn't leading anywhere, anyway. As the noise level rose, I started to think of those occasions when we hear people at the back of the church engaging in a little gossip over the shortcomings of others, when we do well to remember that God knows all there is to know about our sins as well; and he does not permit us to point the finger of judgement at others!

There is so much in church life that is incongruous and funny, and such things are often perceived most readily by new Christians. Drop a brand new believer into a group of stuck-in-the-rut Christians, and innocent but challenging questions begin to be asked about why things are the way they are, and why things happen the way they do. I suspect there may be great delight echoing around the walls of heaven as the enthusiasm of recent converts rattles the cages of routine, indifference and regulation. Newcomers often remind us that God has very odd recruitment policies, too. He seems to think that there may be advantages in calling the rough and ready, the not so clever-minded, the ingenuous, the losers, as well as the educated and outwardly 'successful'. The heavenly Resources Management Department does not seem to be heavily convicted by the necessity for IQ tests, degree qualifications, oodles of money, acres of power or wonderful CVs. God seems to be on the lookout for the simple people who can pull off the big ones for him. His people have included shipbuilders (where there was no sea), plenty of nomads, the odd prostitute now and then, and a number of fairly tricky operators, together with some fishermen, tax collectors and general fanatics. It's not the way most of us would try to run a business or any other organisation! Yet God's 'multi-national' is far greater than any that man has devised.

There can be no doubt about it—God's smile is with us everywhere. He can see the end from the beginning, so he will know when to laugh with us, and when to cry. God knows how often we are preoccupied with the heavy things of life, and longs for us to stand back and see the essential joy, the lighter side, which is usually there to be found, somewhere. The truth is that, whilst Christian teaching may be silent on the matter of humour in God, we *are* told that he is all-knowing, so he possesses intimate knowledge of how we feel and perceive things, including the absurd situations which make us laugh— and in Jesus we see perfect insight into the hearts of all people.

Anyway, rescue was on the way. The twelve year old girl

came running up the aisle and asked, "Can I take Yates with me?"

I handed him over, whispering to her: "What's up?" Well, the church children had been decorating the stage for Christmas, and had neglected to sweep the floor of the building before the service. The place where the dog had enjoyed his pre-worship siesta, rolling back and forth to get comfortable on the hard wooden floor, was covered in glitter—those tiny pieces of silver material that get everywhere! Lying at my feet during the hymn singing was one thing, but the sanctuary searchlights revealed a wonderful sight: a black dog covered in glitter. He looked and shone just like the angel on top of a Christmas tree! Sometimes, God has a wonderful way of taking us down a peg when we're all fired up and ready to go for him. We giggled all the way home!

4

Inside out

The commandments, "Do not commit adultery", "Do not murder", "Do not steal", "Do not covet", and whatever other commandment there may be, are summed up in this one rule: "Love your neighbour as yourself". Love does no harm to its neighbour. Therefore love is the fulfillment of the law.

Romans 13:9

During the first year that Yates and I were together, he was still growing. He was two years old by then, and still thickening out. Our instructors had repeatedly warned us of the dangers of over feeding and generous scrap giving. We had been warned again and again, and were instructed to weigh our dogs at regular intervals. Each record would be checked every six months by visiting instructors, and diets would be adjusted accordingly. In other words, we went home from the training centre in fear of every ounce, every extra inch on the waistline. But Yates was still growing. The maximum weight level quoted in his veterinary record was swiftly exceeded. Was this the thickening out of a maturing dog, or was it plain ordinary fat?

Labradors are well known, perhaps more than most other breeds, for being food orientated. Yates has begging eyes, and a very short memory span, when it comes to suggesting to everyone that he has not been fed today! 'Diet' is a four letter word that he finds quite offensive. His wasp-like waist was beginning to disappear, and his little tummy became more and more obvious. I need not have worried—he turned out to be a beautiful, sleek and shapely animal, fighting fit and raring to go.

Watching him, that first winter's evening as he roasted himself in front of the roaring Christmas fire, I was thankful that his skeleton was on the *inside*. At least he had room to grow. I often teased him in those days by calling him a Vietnamese Pot Bellied Pig, an insult to both species, but I have always been pleased he is not built with his skeleton on the outside! At least he was not a lobster! Lobsters play it safe. They have hard, well-defined, exterior shells because they wear their bones on the outside. Unlike Yates, they have exoskeletons, the scientific word for wearing our hardware on the outside while keeping our tender bits and pieces on the inside. Great protection! Organisms that could be described as having reached a more sophisticated level of development, like me and Yates, reverse this architecture: we keep our hardware on the inside, and wrap our softer tissues tightly around our endoskeleton. Well, in a few little places, Yates' tissues are not always wrapped so tightly, but that's another matter. The 'hard-out-soft-in' principle gives much better protection from predators, which explains why, some five hundred years ago, armour-plated knights coated their bodies, and parts of their horses, in iron, before going into battle. When we can attach some elastic muscle to tough bone, we can do all sorts of interesting things which an exoskeletal cannot manage. A lobster can scuttle along the sand at the bottom of the sea, but he cannot jump up and down, nor can he swing from one tree to another. These different designs are, I suppose, a trade-off between our safety and our potential.

There is a problem, however, with wearing one's skeleton on the outside. If the lobster is going to grow, it is going to have to moult, setting itself free from the hard bit. That is a dangerous business, leaving the poor creature pathetically vulnerable while it remains in the soft, new shell state. No moult—no growth. Thankfully, we endoskeletal types find growth is a slightly smoother and less dangerous affair.

When I started to preach, and more importantly when I started to listen to other people, I found I was retreating within my outer skeleton as rigidly as I could—the skeleton of credal doctrine—not realising what a hard shell this can so easily present to those who need the warmth and understanding of Christ's love displayed to them through other human beings.

I was trying to become a 'lobster Christian'. This way, at least I would get it right according to the Word, or according to acceptable theology. What is more, it cuts down the amount of in-coming flak from other lobsters! It is a safe place to be. It is also a deeply untrustful way to operate. There is another way of ministering, and this is to hold our beliefs as the framework on which to hang our actions: wrapping love, and concern for others, around our core of belief (in the revealed Word of God). This way of operating as a Christian requires a certain amount of trust. It involves holding on to orthodox teaching—which is very important—and also the recognition that we need discernment as to how to apply the truth of Jesus into the lives of those we come across on our way through life. It accepts that credal faith in the revealed Truth is important; but we have to leave room for honest searching, both our own and that of others, as well. It accepts that community is important, and that we Christians have to respect people, with their honest and sincerely held differences. It approaches the world not displaying a sharp, hard outer casing, but with arms opened: with openness and welcome, not with suspicion and mistrust; with respect for others, instead of first insisting that we are right and, all too easily, giving the impression that we Christians have all the answers, when it is only God who does! The depth of damage in so many people's lives means that we need to tend towards the endoskeletal mode when ministering. We must have our beliefs, strong and solidly grounded in the Word of God, but we should surely try not to allow them to be displayed as hard, sharp shell cases, nor insist that we 'know it all'. Too often we begin at the wrong point: trying to use the credal formulae to help other people towards the One who is himself the Truth.

We need to allow our humanity to express the truth to which the creeds bear witness, rather than beat others over the head with our formularies! The point is just that neither creeds nor Scripture, true as they are, were intended to replace personal encounter—and the measure of vulnerability which goes with that—as we come alongside others in the name of the living Lord whom we know. The 'lobster method' may be simple, and seemingly safe and strong—but it does not leave much room for people and for growth, nor for the strength and healing we can find in the Spirit of God.

Our Lord chose to be incarnate on this earth as a human being. He was always spending time with seekers, and sinners, and folk who were hurt and confused. He had far less time for the sort of people who 'knew' what was what and were very clear on law and judgement, and who chose to regard those who were less clear about things than they were as somehow inadequate. He put the way of love before the way of the lawyers, time and again!

5

Casualty

I lift up my eyes to the hills—where does my help come from?
My help comes from the LORD, the Maker of heaven and earth.
He will not let your foot slip
—he who watches over you will not slumber....

Psalm 121:1

Six months of guide dog ownership, and I was on a high with it all. My independence was back; no more ringing up and begging favours—life was free on the 'open road'.

Striding out to work with Yates in the early morning became a joy; listening to the birdsong along the way was an opportunity to join in with the praises from creation. Feet on the ground; head in the heavenlies: wonderful times to be close to God.

Then it happened. Something—I have no idea what it was—made Yates start, and then stumble sideways between my legs. I was jerked around, and fell heavily onto the bank and into the bushes. Two days later found me in our local hospital—one knee in swollen agony—hoping for x-rays and examinations.

I had thought long and hard about this hospital visit. Waiting rooms can be so dreary. Waiting can be boring almost beyond the point of human tolerance. What could I do to seek any preferential treatment? A clergyman's dog collar can be a swift entry passport to hospitals, and I decided to wear one into the casualty department of this one, wondering if it would help now as it had before.

So in we went. My dog collar seemed to throb at my throat, like the anxious attractions of a mating frog in a swamp. Whether we jumped the queue I cannot say, but soon we were ushered into a curtained cubicle. In came the doctor.

"Just drop your trousers and sit on the bed. I'll be back in a moment." Then he was gone. My wife, Ginnie, sat on a chair across the cubicle, while Yates sat on the floor beside me. The scene was too much for Ginnie to bear. The sight of her husband sitting forlornly on the edge of the bed, dog collar around his neck and trousers around his ankles, reduced her to a state of uncontrolled giggling. She could not stop. Yates' reaction reflected his emotions, too. He rested his great head on my dangling left foot as if to say, "I'm so sorry, Dad. This is all my fault."

I just sat there, with Yates, at the bottom of a pit. The mountain top joys of new freedoms seemed long ago, the pleasant valley experiences of the daily round to work and back on my own seemed to have come to an end. Now I was in a desert of hopelessness, wondering if Yates and I would ever get our act together. The doubts and fears for our future crowded in.

Our journeys into the heart of God, just like my journey into new guide dog ownership, are never without hair-raising encounters—with ourselves, and the world around us. God does not allow us to have too many mountain top experiences with him too often, as peaks are fine places from which to look down on others. Neither can we enjoy to the full the air at the mountain top if we have not gasped and struggled for life in the valleys. It may be good for us to be in the deserts of humility sometimes. We cannot, much as we might like to, draw a map of our own escape route from the wilderness experience. We are gently led along the road by God, who has a habit of looking for us in the odder and harder places. It is here, in the wildernesses of life, that our lives are often being shaped by a new found humility, dependence on God, and trust.

Such reforming work does not happen in the valleys, nor on the mountain tops. Thankfully, the heavens are not made of stone: our prayers are always heard. God heard the cry of his people in Egypt, delivering them from their slavery. He went off looking for Elijah in his moment of collapse, dusted him off and put him back on his feet. These thoughts gave me courage, and lifted my soul again, as we waited in the hospital cubicle.

I tried to share my encouragement with Yates: "Come on, my son. It's time we wiped the sand out of our toes, put our sandals—and, indeed, our trousers—back on. It's time to get moving. God and I have quite a few more things for you to do yet!"

Within a month we were back on the road: back with the early morning birdsong, and back with our new freedom. In all the intervening years since the accident, Yates has grown more and more careful, never again dumping me so unceremoniously. He learned a great lesson that day: a lesson about care and caution, about being forgiven and accepted again. I learned something, too. I was beginning to love this dog, despite his one big mistake.

What we *do* in this life makes so little difference, really. What we *are* is everything.

6

Crumbs!

He called out to them, "Friends, haven't you any fish?"
"No," they answered.
He said, "Throw your net on the right side of the boat and you
will find some." When they did, they were unable to haul the net
in because of the large number of fish.

John 21:5

I suppose that Yates is like any other guide dog in that his behaviour is absolutely exemplary—well, most of the time. However, like the disciples in the fishing boat, he will not turn down a potentially fruitful opportunity.

Within a few months of his coming to live with me, I was asked to address a clergy conference held in a hotel one Saturday. Dear Yates was lying down on the speakers' platform for nearly two hours. Under the table, at my feet, he fell fast asleep, while I waited my turn to speak and give my all to the listening crowd. No one would have known he was there.

Lunchtime saw us following the delegates to the back of the hall and into the hotel restaurant, where Yates scootled under the table and went back to sleep. This good behaviour lasted through the mealtime, precisely according to the training manual—and no bother to anyone. I felt really proud of him.

The organisers of the day asked if we would wait a while in the dining room until it had cleared, following lunch. Yates was still sleeping under the table, paws twitching as he 'dream chased' a rabbit across a field. When the dining room had emptied, we followed the delegates back into the conference hall and began to walk sedately through them, towards the platform for the afternoon session.

Something felt wrong. Something definitely was not right with the way Yates was walking; the way he held his head. Exploring with my hand, down his neck and over his face, I came across an enormous bread bun, clasped firmly in his teeth and held high and proud like the spoils of battle. A distinct sense of victory hung in the air! Where did that prize come from? Had he been like the disciples who listened to Jesus, and 'thrown out his net on the right side' for a change? Had he side-swiped it off a passing trolley; or had a crumb fallen from the masters' table, during lunch? However it had happened, Yates had evidently been blessed by this rather large 'crumb'!

Thinking of bread falling from tables reminds us of that remarkable account in the gospels[1] of a woman who came to Jesus to ask for the exorcism of her daughter. Jesus seemed reluctant, at first, to give her what she was asking for—until she spoke of 'crumbs' from the masters' table—crumbs which are eaten by the 'dogs'. The woman was Syro-Phoenician by ethnic identity and Jesus came first to save the Jewish community. He said to her: "I was sent only to the lost sheep of Israel.... It is not right to take the children's bread and toss it to their dogs." What did Jesus mean? He was not referring to our pets, nor to guide dogs! In those days, the Jews had no personal contact with the Syro-Phoenicians. The Israelites were God's chosen people—his children; and all others (pagans) were termed 'dogs'. We recall that a Jewish man would have to undergo a purification rite if he so much as touched a Gentile woman. Most of God's chosen people, certainly the Pharisees and some of the scribes, argued with him, rejecting him as the

---

[1] Matthew 15:21-28; Mark 7:25-30

Son of God. They rejected the Bread of Life. Even his disciples did not understand. Jesus was teaching his disciples here, and he is teaching us: first the chosen, then the dogs. A parallel issue in our own time might be whether one needs to be a Christian to experience healing through Jesus' power.

The woman did not accept 'no' for an answer to her request. She may have been accustomed to having others listen to her opinion—or perhaps this was an inspired interchange with Jesus. Certainly there was no hesitation when she was, initially, rebuffed. She had a response to his apparent refusal, and it was a logical and convincing one. She knew of the 'Son of David'—the Jewish messianic hope—and she had faith that Jesus was that person. While the disciples were clamouring for him to send the woman away, Jesus was communicating with his Father; listening to him. As the woman spoke those words: "Yes, Lord... but even the dogs eat the crumbs that fall from their masters' table", we are shown clearly that she believed Jesus was offering the bread of everlasting life; she knew the value of his word, and she wanted only a scrap. God's chosen children were consistently rejecting the whole loaf, and this woman knew that one small crumb from the Son of God was sufficient to release her daughter from the demonic power, and to give her household God's peace. This woman, her child and her household were powerfully blessed as Jesus spoke those few words of release: "For such a reply you may go; the demon has left your daughter." Even a single crumb of grace can be so healing for any of us.

Now I would have to redeem this situation—somehow. Almost cringing with shame in front of all those church leaders, I yanked away most of the offending object, while Yates swallowed the rest with a gulp that seemed to set up a booming echo around the silent and expectant room. Everyone must have heard it! Still approaching the platform, I was about to turn and face the audience—with a dog in one hand, and a great soggy mass of horridness in the other. What should I do with it? As gracefully as possible, I asked an older gentleman on the front row if he would hold on to something for just a moment, and left it with him. He took it from me without a word, not realising before it was too late that he had become involved in something quite disgusting. What he did with it I shall never know, but I would love to have his thoughts framed on the wall above my desk! On the way home, I reminded a disappointed Yates that the fishermen did not get to eat every fish for breakfast. When grace flows from God, what may seem to us to be only a little is always sufficient.

7

Lost and found

..God was reconciling the world to himself in Christ, not counting men's sins against them.... We implore you on Christ's behalf: be reconciled to God.

2 Corinthians 5:19–20

The terrible day came when Yates went missing. One moment he was lying on the back lawn with a juicy bone between his paws and then, just a little later, when I went outside to find out how he was getting on with it, he was not there any more.

I called and called, but there was no noise of recognition: no jangle of the bells on his play collar. I rushed up the steps to the garden gate, and discovered the problem. Someone had left the gate open. I felt sick in the pit of my stomach. Where had he gone? Would I be able to get him back? Had he gone off with somebody? Would I ever see him again? Had he been caught up into the traffic?

I went out onto the pavement, calling as loudly as I could; I blew the whistle time and time again, trying to blot out the panic, and all those silly alternatives that we dread thinking about on such occasions. I kept on calling for ten minutes. I shouted for him to come home, and I even called him by his alternative name that is often recognised more quickly: "Come on, biscuit!" All was to no avail. Many sorts of emotions crowded in. What would I do if he was hurt? If he could not walk, he would be far too large to carry. What if he never came back? What would I tell the GDBA? How would I manage anything without him? I worried and shouted, and called sweetly, trying every trick I could think of, but nothing worked.

Years before, I had lost an adored pet dog in the same way, and the fear of a repetition of that disaster felt very real. That dog had run down the path at the end of the road and across the busy roundabout at the bottom of the hill. How could I ever forgive myself if Yates had done the same thing? Was he lying somewhere, desperate for my help? Where was he? As a last resort, bearing in mind the importance and value of a guide dog, i resolved to phone the police. I walked miserably back from the roadside to the garden gate and, just as I took the first step, a great black head nudged the back of my knee.

"Is there a problem, Dad?" I felt an instant surge of passionate relief swelling up from my shoes, until it filled my whole body. We went back into the house, and I lay on the floor for over five minutes, with my arms around his neck. I could not be cross with him—it was just such a wonderful relief to have him back with me. My eyes filled with tears. There was nothing else I wanted to do but hold him tight. The 'prodigal dog' had come home.

I thought then of the many times in my life I had sat in churches and heard sermons on that story of the prodigal son, in Luke Chapter 15, when the congregation's attention has been drawn just to the prodigal and his sins—completely missing the real message of the story. We call it the parable of the prodigal son as though the truant were the central character in it. I lay there on the floor, knowing that the important thing here was not that Yates had gone exploring, but what I was feeling. The prodigal son is one of a trilogy of stories that go together—simple tales of a sheep that was lost, a missing coin and a runaway son. The sheep is not central to the first of them—the shepherd is. In the second of these three stories, it is not the coin that the tale is about, but, rather, the housewife who had lost it. It is the loser's pain and the finder's joy that comes under the spotlight in all three stories.

I cannot help thinking that it was our Lord's purpose in telling the story of the prodigal son to concentrate our attention on the father rather than on the sons. It is the pain inflicted on him by the wilfulness of one of his boys, and the other's pride, as well as his joy on the young lad's return, that Jesus wants us to see. Jesus had been taking a great deal of criticism from the Pharisees. In their eyes, he was behaving in a most ungodly way towards such 'undesirable' people as the tax collectors and prostitutes. He seemed to be behaving as if their sins were of no account, and as if God were ignoring all their iniquities. Sinners they might well have been, but as people made by God in his image, he loved them even before they repented. Lying there on the kitchen floor with Yates, my arms around his neck, I could see very clearly that this is the reason why, when we repent, God is so eager to forgive us and receive us back into the family. In the story, the father interrupts the boy's rehearsed confession, and calls for a robe and shoes and a ring before he can finish it. In the society of that day, these things were all marks of sonship. The gift of a robe was a mark of great honour. The ring was a mark of authority: it was the signet ring with which official documents could be signed and sealed. This was actually quite an extraordinary thing for the father to have given. It implied that, without examination or any kind of probationary period, the father trusted him at once with his full authority in all the affairs of the estate. The son could then act in his father's name. It was a mark of complete trust in him. The shoes that the father called for were another mark of sonship. In those days, children were shod, but slaves went barefoot. This, incidentally, was still true in the days of American slavery: hence the Negro spiritual, 'All o' God's chillun got shoes'. In the giving of these three gifts—honour, trust and status—everything was fully restored to the boy, as would befit a true son of the family. I could not see any half measures in the father's welcome.

Nobody listening to Jesus that day would have gone home with the prodigal uppermost in their thoughts. They might even have gone home to talk long into the evening about this extraordinary father that the rabbi had described—a character whom he had surely invented to teach them what was stored up and waiting for them in the heart of God. That is what would have gripped them. There could be no mistaking the meaning of the story. God loves the sinner while he is still a sinner— even before he repents—and that is what makes repentance possible for us, and so worthwhile. This is the passionate yearning in the heart of God, that cannot be quenched even by the wilful persistence of his people in our sinning. It finds its expression, too, in the passion of the Cross. New Testament writers use the word 'longsuffering' to describe it. Peter said that we should hold in high regard the Lord's longsuffering as our salvation, and Paul spoke about it in all his letters. It is the pain God suffers to forgive.

In the story of the prodigal, despite all the grief, all the shame on the family, all the hurt, there must have been burning in the father's heart a flame of love that never dimmed. He ran, nearly tripping over his robes in his childish eagerness. His hands reached out in front of him while he was still ridiculously far from the boy, and, when they met, he embraced him. At last the tears could flow freely, the laughter mixed in with the tears, and through both came the almost choked instructions to the wide-eyed slaves: 'Shoes! Shoes! And a ring; the ring for the son. And the robe; yes, the robe... the best robe.'

'Oh my son, my son, my son.' This is the true nature of God's longsuffering towards us: a great, mountainous, yearning love which is undiminished, despite all the hurt and shame and wounding that has been piled on it. This is what Jesus was seeing in the heart of God as he yearned over the lost and sinning children of men. This was the feeling of intense passion of love's suffering that wrung his own heart as they nailed him to the wood and hung him up. His Cross was only planted on that green hill outside Jerusalem because it had first been reared up in the Father's heart, to deal with our sin.

One of the great privileges of being made in the image of God is that we have the heart ability to feel just a little of how he feels; to cry a few of his tears, and laugh with a few of his joys. What a blessing it was to me that day, to lie on the floor with my friend, my own doggy 'son' and feel a tiny part of what goes on in the heart of God every time I turn around to him and say, "Sorry! Can I come home again?"

8

The Post Office Incident

"See that you do not look down on one of these little ones. For I tell you that their angels in heaven always see the face of my Father in heaven."

Matthew 18:10

In the corner of the Well Centre office is an inviting armchair, which I admit to finding deeply attractive, especially after lunch! While enthroned therein one afternoon, I was invited to visit the post office in the village, to buy stamps. I could say that I was deep in prayer at that point, but checking the inside of my eyelids for holes might have been somewhat nearer the truth! How to find the post office—that was the question.

I got as far as the corner of the right road, and then stopped, clutching the petty cash in my right hand and Yates' harness in my left, praying for an angel to show me the way. In less than five seconds, a man was standing at my elbow. He was making the oft-heard comments about the undisputed beauty of my guide dog.

"Can I help?" he kindly asked. This must have been the angel

I had asked for. I said I needed to know where the post office was and got this reply: "Down there on the left, by the blue car!"

Well, that was not so easy. Down where? What car? A big black dog in a bright, white harness—can you ask for a bigger badge? Would I have to explain?

"I'm sorry," I told him, "I'm blind." There was a long pause, as recognition began to dawn. He was shocked and embarrassed when he realised what he had said.

"I'm really sorry," he said, "I did not realise. Look, the post office is just where that lady in the red dress is going in!" At this point, one has to make choices. A wrong reaction would have been to make a rude response, or to tut-tut, shrugging my shoulders. I could have said nothing and walked on, in the hope of meeting another 'angel'! I could have been gentle, and got into deeper explanations, trying again with him. Perhaps I should have moved the conversation around to Jesus, and asked if they had met, but that did not seem appropriate at the time. A natural human reaction might have been to think, in a superior way, 'how stupid can you get!' In reality I did not find anything to say except 'thanks'. I walked down the road, in the general direction suggested by his comments. What was happening was that I had been tempted to measure the man too harshly. Life is so full of tests, exams and all sorts of measurements that we apply to ourselves and others. We are brought up to measure everybody and everything and most of us seem to be always failing some ideal or somebody else.

Christians have seen the standard set in Jesus, and set higher than any of us can ever dream of attaining. The standard is Christ himself. If we think we can meet that mark, then either we have forgotten that Christ is also God, or we have forgotten that we are not God, we are human. To forget either of these things is a major mistake. At the same time, however, we know that Christ sits with the people at the bottom of the class, which can sometimes be particularly frustrating when we've worked our brains to a standstill to gain a B+.

The fact is that we usually yearn for more credit than we receive. In our humanity, we seek to take pride in our goodness which, too often, seems to mean pointing out how much worse those around us are doing. This was exactly how I was beginning to think about my failing 'angelic' helper.

But we are told very clearly not to do that. This subconscious thought pattern can be our attempt to evade the paradox in the Christian life of failing sinners being set a perfect target. Matthew 9:11 tells us that, when the Pharisees saw what was going on, they asked the disciples why Jesus ate with tax collectors and 'sinners'. On hearing this, Jesus said, "It is not the healthy who need a doctor, but the sick. But go and learn what this means: 'I desire mercy, not sacrifice.' For I have not come to call the righteous, but sinners."

We are all sinners, and all loved, at one and the same time. God asks us to keep both these realities in some sort of tension with each other. That tension is so hard to hang on to; it seems like the hardest work in the world, even though I know that when I came to Christ I became a forgiven sinner!

Paul wrestled with this balance, too. We have the Law, telling us how we all fail, and it is true that God, who is holy, hates sin. We have redemption, through Christ's choosing to die for us; but redemption does not seem to make either the Law or our failure disappear. Neither of them has gone away. Failure is always lurking somewhere. Even the athlete who wins the high-jump competition fails in his final attempt. All high-jumpers fail in the end. We are sinners: that fact is inescapable. But we have God's love, regardless. If we count down from the top, being honest with ourselves about our failures, God counts up from the bottom, holding us like precious jewels in his sight. For every failing we can attribute to ourselves, God recognises and rejoices in another potential diamond for the crown of Christ, and as we become open to the cleansing, purifying work of the Holy Spirit in our lives, we become more like Jesus.

God is such a wonderful Creator! He has designed and built and maintains the universe, and everything in it, in the full richness of colour, shape and form—failing people included. What a boring world this would be if all the trees were the same variety, the same size and the same colour. What a boring place it would be if the people were all the same. The trouble is that I only want God to hear what I want him to listen to. I know that he hears my heart when I worship and when I pray, but if I ridicule someone in my heart, knowing that God sees all that is in there, am I saying in his hearing that he should have made everyone else like me? Oh boy, is that arrogance!

Justice without mercy is not enough. Why cannot we be more merciful to others? We need to pray constantly that our attitudes and responses to those whom we meet will be full of the mercy that Jesus displayed; and we need to ask the Holy Spirit to give us the will and the strength for this to be our heart attitude.

Ah, well. Back to the armchair for more contemplative prayer!

9

Boundary Patrol

A patient man has great understanding,
but a quick-tempered man displays folly.
A heart at peace gives life to the body,
but envy rots the bones.

Proverbs 14:29–30

Guide dog Yates is fond of going out on boundary patrol. This is a daily duty, taking about an hour or so, when he is on the lookout for a suitable hole to clamber through and away. That, I am certain, is the real motive for his journey around the garden—but that is his secret, and he is hanging on to it!

This daily patrol includes a visit to the bottom gate, which will always afford him the opportunity of barking at the passers-by in the village—good sport, apparently. From the diagonally opposite corner of the estate, he can see the faithful and the not-so-faithful calling on the Vicar, who lives next door; and, blessing upon blessing, the Vicar has children who go out to play with balls and things. The excitement of just watching can be quite exhausting for a dog that loves youngsters as much as he does.

From there, it is a short journey along the back hedge to the little iron gate to check out the road down to the village, and then home again. There is only the one boundary in his life, the garden one, but 'the grass is always greener....' One day, there will be a hole in the fence, and then what?

Unlike Yates, we human beings have three sets of boundaries, and most of us are grossly ignorant of all of them most of the time. We cannot see them, nor smell them; we can neither taste nor hear them but, if we come too near, they can really make their presence felt. Break through them, and we may be in trouble. We have a physical boundary known best to joggers as 'the wall'. This can be reached any time during the Sunday afternoon jog, if my long memory serves me right. It takes the unpleasant form of a sort of internal, and almost deafening, scream which demands the jogger stop at once and lie down in the road until the pain passes off. Privately, the real 'success' of the jogger is to break through the wall. When he does, he enters a relatively pain-free world, conscious of his legs revolving underneath him but able to sit back and enjoy the ride, take in the scenery and allow the mind to wander across the open country of the imagination. It's almost an unnatural dream world.

There is an emotional wall, too—less obvious, and therefore more camouflaged from view. It is the dividing line between stress and strain. Stress never killed anyone; but strain? This starts as we get too close to the 'wall', trying to push out the boundaries of our lifestyles to include all we imagine should be in our recipe for success. Approaching this wall feels like headaches, nervous indigestion, high blood pressure, heart attacks and more.

I once read about a small bridge over a river in a rural part of England. A sign on it read 'load limit 10 tons'. It served the local community very well for thirty years or more, with no problems, until a twelve-ton commercial lorry tried to cross it. The additional weight was beyond the bridge's capacity. It collapsed into the river under the extra load.

We are all like that. Each of us has a limit as to how much strain we can handle before we break. It is well documented that too much strain is a killer. Thus we all need to know just how much we can handle, and learn to limit the load we carry. However, while my load limit may be ten or fifteen tons, if I am not flexible and able to bend with the flow, I will collapse and break well below my load limit. No wonder Solomon wrote, "A heart at peace gives life to the body...." So besides limiting the load we take on, we need, as the Bible teaches, to learn how to have a relaxed attitude and to be God-centred in the midst of our stressful and pressured lives: to have that 'heart at peace'. While it is not easy, in a nutshell we need to limit the load we attempt to carry, eat properly, exercise regularly, work hard but take time to relax, laugh at every opportunity, cry when we are sad, never bottle up negative emotions but learn to express them in healthy ways, and let love be our highest aim. Above all, we need to learn to commit and entrust our life to God every day, persevering in prayer, praise and thanksgiving in our hearts, throughout the daily round.

The spiritual boundary, like the other two kinds, has to do with the way God has made us, and is God-given. Much more than the other sorts of boundary, it can sometimes seem to be vague, if not completely invisible; but there are ways to thicken it and make it more solid. We can engage in the study of Scripture, theology and doctrine; have regular fellowship with other Christians, and receive solid teaching. These are some of the 'builder's tools' for maintaining the right kind of spiritual boundary. Without them, we can easily depart—like Yates through that fence—to a place where we are open to heresy and the occult, with all their accompanying dangers.

Yates would love to have his boundaries extended, but the garden is all there is, so it will have to do. We, like him, may sometimes yearn for boundaries of greater circumference. We get fit to extend the physical one, and perhaps we rely on our doctors to allow us to go back and forth through our emotional one with as little pain as possible; but what about the spiritual boundary? The shape and size of that one is the responsibility of the Holy Spirit, and his alone. Only he can demarcate it safely, as he does through the Bible and our conscience; we should allow him to do that 'boundary patrolling' for us.

Thankfully, the dog has returned safely again—cold and wet, but safe. He must have stayed inside the fence today.

10

A Dog with Vision

I do all this for the sake of the gospel, that I may share in its blessings. Do you not know that in a race all the runners run, but only one gets the prize? Run in such a way as to get the prize.
1 Corinthians 9:23–24

On the Saturday before our second Christmas together, the snow arrived in this part of Wales—tons of it. Great thick, wet flakes swirled and drifted down, settling, several inches thick, in the garden; and, on the pavements, swiftly compacting under foot into treacherous, slippery, concrete-like lumps. Yates lay and watched it all, from the warmth and security of his bed.

The timing could not have been better: the increasing likelihood of our having a white Christmas brought a wonderful atmosphere of seasonal joy into the house. In another sense, the timing could not have been worse. Our son and daughter-in-law were on their way from Birmingham, driving down the motorway to spend the festive season in the ageing parental bosom.

By dark they duly and safely arrived in a state of heightened excitement at the sight of all the whiteness. By ten o'clock that night, all pretences at adulthood had flown out of the window, and the old sledge had been retrieved from the garage. Then, in a blizzard of snow flurries, the four of us were up on the hill behind the house, going through our paces in training for the next Olympic bob-sleigh team.

The following morning, Yates, having slept soundly on the idea, put into effect his master-plan to save the world from this cold-white menace. After all, he must have reasoned, human beings are supposed to grow and mature and be enriched by life's experiences, not revert to early childhood at the first excuse! If snow could turn one's respected pack leader into a gibbering six year old, then it would, quite simply, have to go.

Starting work just outside the back door, he took upon himself, without making any song and dance about it, the single-handed responsibility of clearing it all away. All of it! His adopted technique soon became apparent to his amused onlookers, as he metamorphosed into the world's finest snow clearing machine. Large quantities of ice-cold white fluff were taken in at one end of this most efficient piece of food-destroying equipment; converted into warm water somewhere in the middle, and then deposited elsewhere in the garden in the form of steamy little yellow circles on the white crusty surface of the snow.

So far, so good. He had a vision, and he had set out towards it. What's more he was throwing all his God-given talents into the battle; his whole being became absorbed in the task ahead of him. I'm sure he knows the simple truth that a vision without a task is a dream; a task without a vision is drudgery; but a vision and a task together provide hope in the world.

Most of us Christians find it problematic when we wonder about whether or not to do for the Lord something we might not have done before. This is especially so if it means taking on a new venture that looks a little unusual. We ask ourselves whether we could be wasting our time. Is this job just going to be more effort than it's worth? Will I have at least some measure of success?

When we think of Jesus, we remember that after the miracles

in Galilee there came the solitude of the cross. After the proof of God by success, there came the proof of God in what at first appeared to the world as failure: a paradoxical proof perhaps, but how great the effect of that apparent failure has been on the world, in the light of the resurrection.

It is usually difficult for most of us to survive the rigours of either success or failure. Many of us are imbued with an inordinate need to demonstrate our worth through our performance. We long to be luminaries rather than letting our light shine—that is a great mistake that so many of us make. We are, and we want to be, what we *do* and what we *achieve* in life.

On top of all this pressure, which we so often place on ourselves, we have an insatiable appetite for approval. Much of the way in which we drive towards success may well be a veiled means of soliciting compliments. Too many of us spend our waking hours either willing ourselves to succeed or fearing failure. We Christians, like Yates the snow machine, need to be careful of that impostor we call 'success'. We may succeed—but not necessarily in God's way, in which case where is the real and lasting value in what we have done?

Our calling is to do his will, and if he grants us success, fine; if not, then that is fine, too! God's will is that we shall not need to be successful to be happy. If any of us are elated too much by success, or depressed too much by failure, then perhaps we still have some Christian maturing to do!

Ignatius Loyola, who lived from 1491 to 1556, founded the Society of Jesus, known as the Jesuits, on September 27, 1540. This Society was the fulfilment of an all-consuming, lifetime's dream for him. Somebody once asked him how he would feel if the then Pope suppressed the Society (at one point in its early years a real danger).

"A quarter of an hour of prayer," he replied, "and I would think no more of it." He had cultivated, it would seem, a kind of sublime indifference to temporal success or failure.

Watching Yates work, I thought of how his activity modelled that determination to do something without regard for 'success'! When we human beings are setting out on the path of some new venture, the first thing we need is reassurance that we are at least somewhere near doing the right thing at all. The problem here is that failure so often seems almost inevitable in our broken world. We are conditioned to expect it. While we should neither seek failure nor despise success, a Christian is called only to be faithful and obedient—not necessarily successful. The temptation Satan placed before Jesus was what the world might have seen at the time as 'successful' Messiahship—but our Lord chose rather to be a faithful servant, obedient to his Father. Those who cheered Jesus along the road, on that first Palm Sunday, soon had to learn that he was not on his way to a throne in Jerusalem, but to a cross on Golgotha. (And yet the cross was the greatest victory in human history.) Even though we realise this, we still, so often, look for security in many ways.

If Yates had been able to ask people about the validity of his particular vision, he might have met all sorts of responses. Christians might have said, "Wonderful, keep going!", because most of us love to encourage. Cynics would have told him he was wasting his time. Optimists might have said, "Wow! Who can say what a difference you'll make!" Religious people would have exclaimed, "What faith!" and intercessors would have gone away to pray for him. Humanists would have said, "What dogged courage!" A scientist might have advised him to wait for the thaw. A therapist would have asked to check out his puppy-hood; and a realist would most likely have commented, "Stupid dog!" He would have got other people's opinions; but he would have been no nearer knowing whether this action plan was right. He could have sat down and contemplated the pros and cons. Actually, he just *knew* he had to carry out his task. He did not seem to care whether he succeeded or failed; whether he would make a point here about something, set a wonderful example to all of us, or just finish up looking extremely foolish. He just knew what he had to do and he got on with it—quietly, and without fuss or care about the outcome. Did he change the world? Was he successful? Well, all I know is this: there was not a flake of snow left anywhere in the village by Christmas morning!

11

Haircut

"I, even I, am he who blots out your transgressions, for my own sake, and remembers your sins no more."

Isaiah 43:25

Haircut days are good days for Yates: there is always a blessing or two in store. The route from home to Roddy's hairdressing salon is well known to him, though its early stages are fraught with alternatives. Two roads have to be crossed, instead of corners turned, and other routes branch away to other destinations. A quarter of a mile into the trek and he knows what is happening: all the alternatives have passed. If Dad goes this way, then there can only be one possible ending to the trip—the girls in Roddy's salon! Finding the right door to the right shop is an old guide dog skill. Yates needs to be told on entering a new shop what the name of the establishment is. Two or three goes at this and he remembers for ever.

Giving the command "Find Sainsbury's!" or "Find the chemist!" is all that is required to ensure safe arrival at the right place. Roddy's initially presented Yates with a problem. The New Age shop just this side of the salon has exactly the same type of frontage, the same make of front door. Even now, after much practice, he still sometimes gets the wrong entrance.

Guide dogs are trained to take initiative in harness and to follow their instincts, which, in Yates' case, usually means pausing just inside the shop doorway to seek my approval. The command "Not today, thank you!" will initiate reverse thrust and we are back out on the street—but not with this particular shop. Once inside, Yates smells the unusual smells, hears the unusual music, recognises the absence of hair dryers and takes himself, and me, out of there as fast as he can. There is no waiting to check with Dad; his reaction is immediate. What discernment!

Once safely into Roddy's salon, the fun starts. If we have timed it right and there is a short lull in the flow of business, Yates swiftly becomes covered in girls. This is good; the ears are fondled, the top of his head is scratched. The back comes in for the standard rubbing procedure, and then it is time to roll over. Once the chest is offered up, then bliss arrives!

Ah well, good things never seem to last long for the average guide dog. Dad has to go and sit in the chair to get his own share of attention. Yates dutifully curls up at my feet, under the counter and out of harm's way, keeping an ever watchful eye out for the girls, in case they have another free moment.

Then the cutting begins: first the beard trimming and then the rest. By the nature of things, the discarded hair falls to the floor and mixes with any leftovers from previous clients. Now Yates sets to work. Puffing short breaths out of his nostrils, he begins to push the hair around on the floor. At first I thought he was trying to clear his nose from some invading tickle, but this activity is far from that, and was quite unexpected.

"What's going on down here?" I asked Roddy, the first time it happened.

"Well," he said, "you wouldn't believe it! He's actually separating your beard hairs from all the rest and then eating them! How sweet!"

Why? It was all just hair, after all. Yet there he lay, softly blowing away anything he did not want, until he was left only with his heart's desire, which he then took into himself.

This made me remember the work of Jesus and the work of the Holy Spirit today, softly separating the good from the not-so-good within me. Once again, I thought of the wonderful truth that I am 'in Christ' and he is 'in me': something that is true for every believer.

I began to hum the tune of 'Amazing Grace'.

> *Amazing grace how sweet the sound*
> *that saved a wretch like me.*
> *I once was lost, but now am found,*
> *was blind, but now I see.*

John Newton was living out this famous hymn long before he wrote it. Describing himself as a libertine, he recognised no God to whom he should count himself responsible. He made his living for a while as a slave trader, before the Holy Spirit showed him both his sin and his Saviour. In his own epitaph he wrote: "Here lies John Newton, Clerk, a libertine and former slave trader, who was, by the rich mercy of God, redeemed and appointed to proclaim the faith he had long laboured to destroy." When he grew to be an old man with a fading memory, a friend urged him to give up preaching. Newton answered him, "My memory is nearly gone; but this much I remember: that I am a great sinner, and that Christ is a great Saviour."

We stand before God as the whole human race. What was said of our ancient ancestors is still true of us, today. We were born in the reflection of Adam, and we have the stain of original sin upon all our lives. We are sinners. God is both just and gracious, and he must uphold his justice. Does he do that?

Imagine how we would feel if a judge was appointed to the Bench, who then never sent anyone to jail. Society would be outraged. Like any judge, God must punish us in our sin to be just, but he does not want to. That is why he sent Jesus.

God presented him as a sacrifice of atonement, through faith in his blood. He did this to demonstrate his justice, because in his forbearance he had left the sins committed beforehand unpunished—he did it to demonstrate his justice at the present time, so as to be just and the one who justifies those who have faith in Jesus.

Romans 3:25

Yates' work of separating out the debris in the salon brought to mind another biblical picture of the work God does for all who are redeemed and forgiven, sweeping away everything in us that we let go, as we turn away from the things that grieve him.

"I have swept away your offenses like a cloud, your sins like the morning mist. Return to me, for I have redeemed you."

Isaiah 44:22

How good and infinitely worthwhile it is to know that the softly sweeping hand of the Holy Spirit is doing a work of sanctifying, purifying, refining in our lives; because, ultimately, God will have taken away all that is not for him; he is changing me, by his grace. In the end, at the general resurrection, as Paul teaches us, we shall be changed. But that is a process which has already begun.

The route home has one essential ingredient—a visit to the post office in the village. Here, Yates can expect at least two sweets, his just reward, just because he is the dog he is.

12

Inspection

Peter, an apostle of Jesus Christ, To God's elect, strangers in the world, scattered throughout Pontus, Galatia, Cappadocia, Asia and Bithynia, who have been chosen according to the foreknowledge of God the Father, through the sanctifying work of the Spirit, for obedience to Jesus Christ and sprinkling by his blood: Grace and peace be yours in abundance.

1 Peter 1:1–2

Every six months, as regularly as clockwork, the phone rings. It is inspection time again. Guide dogs are trained to the highest level in social, obedience and guiding skills. At the moment they pass into the hands of the would-be guide dog owner, at the point where the partnership begins, they are at the very peak of their training.

Few stay that way. They are trained by experts, and then managed by owners who are often tempted to let them get away with little things, just now and again. So, twice a year, the GDBA instructors put the dogs through their paces once more, polishing them back up to scratch.

The impending visit always precipitates a visit to the vet—not one of Yates' favourite pastimes! A complete health check is carried out and recorded. Eyes, ears, teeth, heart, lungs and stomach, all are examined; all is written down. Then the appointed day arrives.

"How's he keeping?"

Yates' health record is examined. I imagine some eyebrow twitching or frowning invading the instructor's face as she reads his weight, and get ready to calm her down.

"Would you like a cup of coffee?"

Next, Yates is saddled up and off we all go to the town to show off his crowd skills, his off-kerbs and on-kerbs, his far traffic knowledge and all those incredible talents which instructors understand much better than we do! Approaching the middle of the town, on one such occasion, my instructor called out from behind me.

"Go straight on to the end of the building line and turn left. If we then take the first left and come back on ourselves, I can go to Marks and Spencer to collect something I need!"

Yates did not hesitate. Turning sharply to his left, he took us up the side route, the short cut to the department store. Straight in through the doors he trundled, without waiting for instruction. Turn left, turn right, and along to the Customer Enquiries desk, where he stopped. Turning his head to me, he almost said, "Hey, Dad, how's that?"

The instructor was a little perplexed. She had fully expected us to follow her instructions, and thought I had cheated by taking the short cut.

"It's Yates," I told her. "You said Marks and Spencer and he knows where that is!" This dog is so clever that he is nearly perfect. His master, however, is a long way from the perfection and holiness of Christ, longing for it so that he might one day become a vehicle for the display of his own master's splendour.

Holiness takes a lifetime to grow, and is primarily a gift of God. We were, initially, made holy or 'set apart for God' by God's Spirit, when we came to Christ. This is not something we have done for ourselves, in the first instance. Indeed, if we read Peter correctly, the overall impression we get is that we become holy in practice because we were first 'made holy'. We become what we are. In his book on spirituality, entitled *The Pure in Heart*, Sangster writes:

> It is a religious rather than an ethical order. The New Testament does not call people 'holy' because they are righteous but because they are becoming righteous by the indwelling of the Holy Spirit. The Holy Spirit indwells them, in order to make them holy. And that is the way of it. The utterly impossible in righteousness is made gloriously possible by the life of God in the soul of a human person.

Just as those Old Testament priests, and even their ceremonial utensils, had 'holiness unto the Lord' written on them, so do we, the Church of Jesus Christ. This is the calling, the vocation, of the whole Church. No one need be left out. We are all called to be holy. God sent his son, Jesus, to us, to create a new people—new men, new women, new young people and children, who are to be so different from others that they can be called 'holy' and 'pure'.

We should be setting out each day making every effort to live in peace with everyone we meet and to be holy. Without holiness no one will see the Lord. So what is stopping us? Why is it that other people look at us and do not see an image of Christ straight away? It is because, in a picture I find helpful, we are like lampstands. These lamps have a base, which may be thought of as representing the body. They also have a light bulb, which needs a two-core cable, connecting the whole to the mains supply. One core carries our worship to God and the other is the power supply of his Love for us. It has a switch that we may think of as the new birth or Baptism of the Holy Spirit, and that switch has on it the hand of Jesus. As he moves the switch, the bulb becomes alight with his glorious Light. God promises to put a new Spirit within us. How the light shines when God does this work in a new believer, or a believer in whom is renewed his or her first love for Jesus!

Covering the bulb is a lampshade, which comes in a complete range of colours and patterns and differing thicknesses, all of which soften, discolour, darken and sometimes altogether obliterate the glow. The lampshade represents our sinful nature, and the distorting effect—the pattern—is formed as a result of our sins, our reactions to past wounds, our hang-ups and sometimes our contrary will.

God the Father has sent the Holy Spirit as a gift to the Church to deepen our relationship with himself through Jesus; and, by the help of his healing grace, to increase the transparency of our 'lampshades', so allowing his light to shine in us more and more. This grace is not just about healing diseases; it is to enable us to walk humbly with God, together with other Christians, ever further along the road towards our wholeness in him.

It is not so much that *others* need to grow to make the Church holy; it is rather that *I* need to grow in holiness; and that means I need to allow God to do more of what he wants to do in me.

Back at the house, Yates, exhausted by the stresses and strains of showing off his 'near perfection', collapsed asleep in his basket.

"All I can say is this," began the instructor. "He's a star!"

13

Falling and Failing

Now we pray to God that you will not do anything wrong. Not that people will see that we have stood the test but that you will do what is right even though we may seem to have failed.

2 Corinthians 13:7

It was just lovely to stretch out on the dry grass under the July sunshine and close my eyes. I had been working hard, helping to lead a week-long residential Christian holiday for about a hundred folk who had come to enjoy themselves in beautiful Devonshire.

Yates was lying with me, his back tucked into my side, showing no signs of life other than the usual ever-twitching nose. We had half an hour. Then would come the concert, with my co-leader, Marilyn Baker, that wonderfully gifted international Gospel singer. I was so looking forward to being there to listen. Yates would have to spend yet another evening keeping a watchful eye on Giles, Marilyn's guide dog. Twenty-five minutes to go; time for a little snooze in the warmth of the early evening sun. I was woken by the strains of glorious music wafting across the lawn from the concert room.

"Wake up, my son, we'll be late!" I called, leaping to my feet, still in a doze. I reached out for the lead to put around his neck but there was no dog! 'Dog-gone', as the Americans might say. At this point, the experienced guide dog owner simply and coolly reaches for his whistle. Three quick blasts and the dog would be at my side. Well, that's what they teach at the guide dog training centre. This particular guide dog owner simply panicked!

All his young life, Yates had been brought up with the whistle. Every mealtime, his food had been placed in front of him while he sat and waited for the desired notes. Three toots and he could start eating. The logic of all this training is easy to follow, Yates grew up associating the sound of the whistle with food. As not much else figures in his life, except his Dad, he is trained to respond to the idea that three quick blasts means that food might be available. Well, that's the theory. In practice, it all depends. Yates does not obey like a machine, he works it out. The question he has to ask himself is this: is what he has at that precise moment more interesting than anything Dad might have? If the answer is no, then recall is immediate. If the answer is yes, then Dad will have to wait.

So I blew again. And again, and again. This regrettable state of affairs continued for over ten minutes—and still no dog. Where on earth had he got to? Just then, the doors of the concert room burst open, and out ran four or five worried souls. "What's up? Has Yates disappeared?"

They split up, vanishing in different directions to scour the gardens for him. In only a few minutes one came back, running across the grass and hanging on for dear life to his collar. Yates jumped up at me, his wagger propelling him like a rear-engined aeroplane. He was thrilled to see me and longing to tell me about all his adventures. Should I welcome him back, or scold him for being a failure? Certainly God would welcome me back under similar circumstances, so I did the same.

On with the harness, on with the lead, and into the concert room we crept, to find the performance stopped and the entire audience waiting for us. Up went the cheer as we entered, and up went all the blood into my cheeks as I stood there and cringed. How embarrassing!

"Yates," I gritted through my teeth, "now you've done it, you've really fallen from grace!" As we took our seat he placed his head between my knees and pushed. He knew, then, that he had been naughty, but as he often does on such fallen occasions, he overcame his apparent disgrace by looking up at me and 'smiling'. As I 'forgave' my dog for his moment of disobedience, I was reminded of God's lesson for me:

> Consider it pure joy, my brothers, whenever you face trials of many kinds, because you know that the testing of your faith develops perseverance. Perseverance must finish its work so that you may be mature and complete, not lacking anything.   *James 1:2–4*

Jesus told his followers that they would experience three things: joy that no one would take away from them;[1] trouble while in this world;[2] and his indwelling presence.[3] We modern people have been seduced into thinking that if only life were to be properly organized, it could be trouble-free. Yet the truth is that the trials of life are to be used positively. The testing of our faith is to make us become people who persevere.

"So, Lord," I prayed, as everyone else got involved in the concert again, "just as you did not cast off your people who failed in the past, but forgave them, restored them, and re-commissioned them, so now I, too, accept your grace. Remind me anew that while failure is always possible, failure is not final. Thank you, Lord, for showing me that all my fallen moments can be redeemed."

But why was it that so much attention was being paid to Yates' disobedience by the entire audience in this concert hall? It emerged that the high pitched whistle had somehow embedded itself in Marilyn's sound system, striking horror into the heart of her sound engineer—so much so that she had to stop the concert until the elusive problem could be found and mended. It was only when he, too, began to fail in his search for the virus in the system that someone had suggested that my guide dog whistle might be the culprit.

What could I do but take hold of Yates' ears and bless him?

[1]See John 16:22   [2]See John 16:33   [3]See John 14:20

14

Seeking

So do not throw away your confidence; it will be richly rewarded.
You need to persevere so that when you have done the will of
God, you will receive what he has promised.

Hebrews 10:35

There are times when visions from God—his ideas given to us—
seem vague and empty of detail, often so empty of direction
that we have no idea how to make a start. Sometimes, there is
just a hint of something in the air and sometimes, so Yates tells
me, just a slight smell under the nose. I am sure there is a
reason for this apparent 'vagueness'. Part of any act of
obedience is working out the best way, in God's eyes, of
completing the task set before us. And the perseverance of a
dog with a smell under his nose is something to behold and a
lesson to learn!

I had been invited to preach at a healing service, and to
participate at the communion rail with the ministry team at
the end of the service. It had been a long drive to get there and
I was tired, praying for the enthusiasm for a good preach. Yates

had spent the three hour journey asleep on the back seat of the car and was annoyingly fresh on arrival. We entered the church, and I spoke with those welcoming us at the door, to make sure we were in the right place; and then I gave Yates that useful guide dog command, "Find a seat!"

Down the aisle we went, a one-dog, one-man procession to the front of the pews. This would be good: a seat on the front bench; easy access to the place from where I would have to deliver the words that I had just been given to say. But Yates did not stop. Past the front pew we went and on up into the sanctuary and, plonk, there I was, enthroned in the Bishop's chair! He's made this move before and since, and I can only pray that it is not prophetic!

A few weeks earlier, I had been giving a talk in Salisbury Cathedral and Yates had walked in and taken me straight to the speaker's chair without having been asked to do so. He knew, that time, where I had to go. A man in the audience called out, "How sweet! He thinks you're the speaker!" I was.

So here in this church we sang and talked and preached, and the time came to go back up towards the altar and prepare for ministry. At least this time we went up to the altar when *I* wanted to, and not when the dog did. For some reason known only to Yates, not only does he sometimes take me to the Bishop's chair, sometimes it is straight to the altar at the beginning of a service. This can be extremely embarrassing when I am not officiating! The installation of one yard high altar rails was first insisted upon in the seventeenth century by Archbishop Laud, precisely to prevent dogs from approaching the altar; an act considered in those days to be deeply irreverent. Since then, the rails have become more open and lower affairs, presenting no obstacle at all to the modern determined canine member of the congregation. Through this particular rail we went and, having turned me around to face the congregation, Yates subsided with a sigh onto the floor, falling back into a deep sleep.

The leads that are issued with guide dogs are double length. They have a spring clip which releases the leather strap into twice its otherwise normal length. I unclipped the spring catch and attached it to the belt of my trousers. This releases me to move more freely as the people come forward. For half an hour we prayed with the considerable number who came up. Then it happened. Just as the last seeker after God's grace turned back towards the pews, the belt began to tighten around my waist—gently at first, and then a little more persistently, I was drawn towards the altar. Was this some spiritual attraction? Was I now to be raptured into heaven? Was I feeling some priestly draw towards the altar of God? No, it was Yates. A smell was under his nose, and he was filled with confidence about it. I could not pin-point the source of any aroma, but he could. His sights were set on some apparent 'gift', and he was determined. He needed to persevere, so that when he had followed the smell under his nose, he would receive what he believed was promised. But what *was* so promising? What was it that, in his mind, had become of greater importance than the occasion? I was reminded of the way in which a Christian sometimes senses that God has a gift or blessing to give, and we begin to go for it—to seek it from him.

By the time I had fully applied the brakes, I caught a fuzzy but wonderful sight out of the edge of one eye. On the communion table were some flowers, a brass cross and two candlesticks. A great white cloth, which covered the table, reached down to the floor. In full view of everyone there was a great black backside protruding out into the church. The front end was lost to sight under the altar cloth. Back and forth across the face of the white cloth travelled a black windscreen wiper, known in the guide dog business as a wagger. Something under there was pretty good.

I wondered what the Vicar had been up to and began to think of those ancient days in the Temple, when pigeon killing would have been a continuous affair. What had been going on here? What had been left under the altar which so attracted Yates? I felt a hundred eyes behind me as I faced up to the situation. Would the moment be lost? How does one behave with grace under such circumstances? With both hands on the lead, I began to pull, throwing my whole weight against the great persistence of a dog following his nose into the unknown. This was no occasion to shout the command 'Leave it!' I could only pull. Eventually, Yates backed out from under the altar cloth, only to stare at me with a certain lack of understanding. I never did discover what it was that had so engaged Yates, leading him to embark on his exploration in such an enthusiastic and determined way.

All those good people in the congregation who had come to the healing service, seeking something of the love-mercy of God, received grace from the Lord, who was faithful to his promise to be there with us; and yet, when it came to Yates, he had been forced to abandon his quest for whatever it was *he* was after.

His little escapade, so marked by persistence and a good measure of endurance, reminded me that there are times when all the blessings that God has in store for us seem to be just out of reach. Stretch out for them as we may, we sometimes fail to grasp them. This is not because the gifts, or the Giver, are not real. It is usually because we collapse in a heap of self-pity when we could have been struggling on towards him.

We should never throw away our confidence in Christ; it will be richly rewarded. We need to try and try again, so that when we have done the will of God, we will indeed receive what he has promised.

15

Thorns

I want to know Christ and the power of his resurrection and the fellowship of sharing in his sufferings, becoming like him in his death, and so, somehow, to attain to the resurrection from the dead.

Philippians 3:10

Sitting opposite me, on the sofa in one of The Well Centre's ministry rooms, was an eighty year old lady in floods of tears. Just for once, I had not said a word for an hour; she had talked non-stop, pouring out her life story, as all the badness and the horror of it piled into the front of her memory. There were things she thought she had forgotten, and stories she had never told anyone before.

She spoke of being bombed in London in the war, and of evacuation to Wales as a young girl; of growing up alone in a strange country without childhood friends, and of strings of broken relationships. She told of teenage violence and drug abuse, of rape and three disastrous marriages, together with a seemingly endless story of miscarriages and stillborn babies.

There seemed no end to her tragedy. I marvelled at the strength of a human being, that she could endure so much and yet still survive. I let her talk and talk until she could do so no more. Worn out with crying, she eventually shrank and collapsed back into the cushions, with her knees tucked up under her chin. There was a minute's pause in the conversation and then, out of the blue, she said, "Mind you, I would hate to go blind. I can put up with most things in life, but not that—I think I would kill myself." I was shocked.

Yates stirred on the carpet between us. Large though he may be, he has a wonderful ministry knack of keeping out of the way when he needs to, and of sometimes stretching to his feet and wandering over to sit against the legs of some hurting person at the right moment. In the silent pause between us, he lifted up his great head and looked at the old lady. One eyebrow raised itself in question. Then he stood and stretched, coming over to sit at my feet. It was my turn, this time.

Staring up at me with the other eyebrow too high on his forehead, he seemed to be asking me, "Why do other people's thorns always seem unbearable, and our own do not seem to be so bad?" He pushed his head into my knees in reassurance. "We're OK, aren't we, Dad?"

Afterwards I thought of George Matheson, who was born in Glasgow in 1842. Although he had been born with poor eyesight, he was able to go to Glasgow University. During his time there as a student, his sisters worked with him by transcribing all his ideas onto paper and reading all his text books to him. After graduating with a master's degree, his eyesight deteriorated to total blindness. He served as a pastor for over thirty years at three different churches, having the ability to memorise his sermons and recite large passages of Scripture. Other pastors around him praised his sermons for having so much spiritual freshness. This is the prayer that he wrote about not being able to see:

My God, I have never thanked Thee for my thorn! I have thanked Thee a thousand times for my roses, but never once for my thorn; I have been looking forward to a world where I shall get compensation for my cross as itself a present glory. Teach me the glory of my cross; teach me the value of my thorn. Show me that I have climbed to Thee by the path of pain. Show me that my tears have made my rainbow.

Thorns vary from the unpleasant to the almost unbearable, but they are often used to assist our spiritual growth. We can learn much about the glory of Christ's Cross when we understand the purpose of our own thorns. Had she ever thanked the Lord for the thorns in her own life? Is it too crazy a thing to suggest that we should thank God for thorns? Well, maybe so, for after all Paul tells us that he pleaded with the Lord repeatedly—three times, in fact—for his 'thorn in the flesh' to be taken away from him.[1] But we can thank God for the lessons we learn along the way about the glory of the Cross, and we are to 'give thanks in all circumstances'.[2] We can thank the Lord that he has used the thorns to help keep us dependent on him. We can thank God, too, that he will remove them one day, for all eternity.

The phrase, 'growing strong in the broken places' helpfully conveys the idea that where a bone is broken and then heals, that place becomes the strongest part of the bone. The same is true of our broken places—where we have been hurt, have fallen or failed. When we bring these to Christ for his healing, his strength is then made perfect in and through our weaknesses. The healing power of Christ turns our thorns into roses. Ministering to other people, I have so often seen this to be true. They are helped, not through the minister's brilliant logic, shimmering theology or persuasive talking, but through speaking of our struggles and how God's help has enabled us to overcome them. It is a case of one beggar showing other beggars where to find bread. The Lord said to the Apostle Paul, "My grace is sufficient for you, for my power is made perfect in weakness."[3] So it is that Paul affirms, "..we know that in all things God works for the good of those who love him, who have been called according to his purpose."[4]

Meanwhile, in the ministry room, Yates' head still rested on my knee. I sat in my chair in complete silence, tongue-tied at the mere thought that this lady could even consider my thorn

[1] See 2 Cor. 12:8   [2] 1 Thess. 5:18   [3] See 2 Cor. 12:9   [4] Rom. 8:28

to be on the same scale of measurement as all her troubles, let alone a more vicious kind of suffering.

It was the dog who made the right move. He looked up at me as if to ask my approval for something, and then turned to look at the old lady on the sofa. Whatever the argument about whose thorns were the nastier ones, the real question to him was where the greatest pain was in the room. That is not a difficult decision for a wise old guide dog. Stepping across the ministry room carpet, he sat quietly at her feet, pushing his black nose into her lap.

At the same moment, in the form of unconditional love, Jesus came to be with her.

16

Blackdog's Revenge

Then Peter came to Jesus and asked, "Lord, how many times shall I forgive my brother when he sins against me? Up to seven times?"

Jesus answered, "I tell you, not seven times, but seventy-seven times."

Matthew 18:21

Hanging on the fence by the old imposing wooden gate to the churchyard was a freshly painted sign which read: 'No Dogs Allowed'. Well, that was understandable, I suppose. Who wants other people's doggy visiting cards left all over their church-yards?

But why then were there two horses among the less cared for graves, happily chewing their way through yards of unkempt grass, blissfully unaware that their visiting cards would almost certainly have been a little more apparent than those left by the average guide dog? Yates stopped for a moment and stared at them, obviously trying to work out the missing pieces of logic in the scene before him. After a lengthy pause it seemed as though he had decided that guide dogs were sufficiently superior to anything else on four legs that no one could possibly argue about his presence. Off he set along the tarmac path towards the church doors.

We were going to a service—well, some sort of ceremony, of a kind that we had not been to before. It was a five-yearly official inspection and renewing of Licences by the Bishop and the Registrar; a legal, rather than a worshipful, occasion. Following the principle that the last will be first, and the first will be last, we sat down in a pew at the back of the church. Actually, this manoeuvre has an added advantage: it allows a dog to stretch out all over the floor, without tripping up too many passers-by.

This time, Yates decided on another plan. The church was so cold that he hunted out a tepid pipe under the pew, and then huddled against it, whimpering something about how we should try to warm up our churches before we pay too much attention to such out-reaching things as mission and evangelism. After the singing time and the preaching time came the queueing. The line of people ran from the front to the back of the large, icy building, and the people applying for re-endorsement were stacked three or four wide down the centre aisle: more than a hundred of them. Was this the queue, or were they all just huddled together for warmth? Yates has to decide these things for himself. We did not want to miss the queue by going to the wrong collection of bodies. That sort of decision takes quite a bit of discernment for a dog and, by the time he had made up his mind, we were right at the back and nearly the last to move forward. Yates was calm, steady as a rock at the impending wait. Two hours he stood there, inching forward little by little, as those at the front were peeled off and dealt with. Two hours of growing leg ache and shivering back strain passed by, until eventually we reached the front. By now, Yates had seen enough of all this. First a racist sign forbidding his entrance, and now a hundred people to prevent him from progressing. What next?

At last the Bishop took my Licences and leaned towards the be-wigged Registrar, whispering something in his ear. Perhaps it was too secret and lofty for mere mortals like me to grasp.

Then he sat back and said, "Hello, Mike. I'm afraid there's a problem. You haven't brought all your Licences with you; there's one missing." I swear there was a definite clatter, as my heart fell into one of my boots, quickly followed by another sound as Yates' heart fell into his. Had we not suffered enough? Were our trials and tribulations in vain? First the indignation and rejection at the gate and then the ice-cold waiting for hours, and now it was all wasted. We would have to go home in failure and try again another day.

"Which one's missing?" I tentatively enquired.

"The dog licence," came the straight-faced reply.

Humans have a wonderful capacity for summoning up a weak laugh and a polite smile when everything inside is screaming. Dogs are far more forgiving, and as wise as serpents. Both these are good Christian virtues, but I was about to witness the black guide dog's dark revenge. Gracefully, gently, with big eyes and just the hint of a smile, Yates inched his chin up onto the edge of the Bishop's table.

"Hello, Yates, how are you?" The question was taken as encouragement to move on with the plan. The front paws were off the ground now, and his chest was resting on the table's edge. As charming as ever, he stretched and stretched towards his Bishop, ostensibly eager to say hello.

Suddenly, the truth dawned on me; too late, I grasped Yates' plan for revenge.

"Oh dear," sighed the Bishop, "that's the end of my biscuit!"

"Gotcha!" thought Yates, pulling back down onto the floor and swallowing hard. "Revenge is sweet!"

We left hurriedly, feeling that we had, somehow, brought a spirit of rebellion into the otherwise serious and sombre proceedings. By the churchyard gate we stopped; it was time for me to do some teaching of my own.

"Yates, 'you shall not steal', Exodus 20:15. Oh, and while I'm about it, 'Do not take revenge, my friends, but leave room for God's wrath, for it is written: "It is mine to avenge; I will repay," says the Lord,' Romans 12:19."

The black head turned slowly sideways towards me, and a condescending look oozed at me out of the corner of his eye, as I thought of another verse: 'The thief comes only to steal and kill and destroy; I [Jesus] have come that they may have life, and have it to the full!' (John 10:10).

Never let it be said that Yates does not know how to get the best out of a bad situation. We all fall into them from time to time: any sort of place between frustration and tragedy. But in all of them is a little piece of gold from God, lying there and waiting to be picked up and realised. In all sufferings there are blessings, and even the search for them lifts the soul.

Living life to the full, even in times of hardship, is high on the Yates' priority list, especially if it wins him a biscuit!

17

The Evangelist

As you go, preach this message: 'The kingdom of heaven is near.'
Heal the sick, raise the dead, cleanse those who have leprosy,
drive out demons. Freely you have received, freely give.
Matthew 10:7–8

There must be a thousand wonderful ways in which Yates has
been of support to me and to my ministry. Helping me to open
up, to go more public with myself, has been one of them. He is
such a marvellous conversation starter. Sometimes these are
good talks with people, and sometimes they are not so good.
But minute-by-minute opportunities were far fewer before the
days of Yates.

Christians need to be open before others about their faith.
The Church is such a shy organization. Having a vehicle to
start conversations for one is a great gift! Not everyone has a
guide dog, but we all have something—some aspect of our
lives—that we can offer to God for the furtherance of his
kingdom. One older evangelist in the church told me recently,
"Growing old isn't so bad after all. I don't have to *do* anything;

it just happens. Of course, there are aches and pains, but even they help my social life. We all hurt all over, so the subject is never exhausted!"

Christianity is not private; it is essentially evangelistic. Jesus was sent from heaven to earth. He walked everywhere, meeting people and sharing his good news. He has instructed us all to share the Kingdom, as we go about our daily business. We are not brought into the Church to hide our beliefs in a corner.

Our lives are filled with opportunities; we have only to find them. Our own suffering is an important holder of our potential witness. Oswald Chambers wrote:

> There is no such thing as a private life, a world within the world, for a man or a woman who is brought into fellowship with Jesus Christ's sufferings. God breaks up the private life of his saints and makes it a thoroughfare for the world, on the one hand, and for himself on the other. No human being can stand that unless he is identified with Jesus Christ. We are not sanctified for ourselves; we are called into the fellowship of the Gospel and things happen that have nothing to do with us. God is getting us into fellowship with himself. Let him have his way. If we do not, instead of being the slightest use to God in his redemptive work in the world, we will be a hindrance and a clog. The first thing that God does with us is get us based on rugged reality until we do not care what becomes of us individually as long as he gets his way for the purpose of his redemption. Why shouldn't we go through heartbreaks? Through these doorways, God is opening up ways of fellowship with his son. Most of us fall and collapse at the first grip of pain; we sit down on the threshold of God's purpose and die away of self pity, and all so-called Christian sympathy will aid us to our death bed. But God will not; he comes with the grip of the pierced hand of his son and says, "Enter into fellowship with me. Arise and shine!"

Yates sat patiently at the kerb, watching the traffic coming up the hill from our right. Just at the moment when he spotted a safe gap in the traffic and got to his feet, the lollipop lady strode up to him.

"Good afternoon, Yates!" she said to him. He sat down again at the kerb. 'Look out,' he must have recognised the moment. 'Here's another one for Dad!'

"Isn't he lovely?" She paused as she bent to stroke his head.

"Oh look," she added, "he's even got a halo!"

"Yes," I joked with her, "perfect for a Christian's dog!" Back in the kitchen with my ministry partners, I told them of her comment. They, too, came to wonder at this 'holy' sight. It was not a halo, it was egg yoke. I had been for a late breakfast in the local café and Yates had been the main beneficiary of the trip. As I dug my knife into the sausage, my fork had slipped and flicked my fried egg off the plate. It sailed through the air, falling between my knees, straight onto the sleeping black head resting on my right foot. Yates had moved like a striking snake. Thanks to his immaculate skill and timing, the egg rose in response to a deftly jerked head, then fell back into the open mouth that was waiting for it. One swallow, followed by a sigh of satisfaction, and his head gently fell back onto my foot. God moves in mysterious ways. Even the remains of an egg yoke can become a halo to someone!

So on I go, just walking with God in front and behind; trusting him and being at peace that I am going the right way for him. As Yates in his way was ready for whatever might happen, I want to be ready and attentive for what God may do. This is a verse which helps me to go on expecting great things from God:

Then your light will break forth like the dawn, and your healing will quickly appear; then your righteousness will go before you, and the glory of the LORD will be your rear guard.

Isaiah 58:8

18

The Beam

...our gospel came to you not simply with words, but also with power, with the Holy Spirit and with deep conviction. You know how we lived among you for your sake....

1 Thessalonians 1:5

Lent is probably a time of mixed blessings for the average guide dog. It certainly has been for the one that lives with me! On the one hand has been the repentant life. The subject of the need to diet has come up once too often for his taste, and the subject of personal holiness has not sparked his interest at all. *But* there have been high moments. One Teaching Day lunchtime at The Well Centre provided him with the sight of people wandering around clutching biscuits and pieces of cake. Once the possibility of a potential target has been realised, his 'Tractor Beam' is switched on. Devotees of *Star Trek* will know a 'Tractor Beam' when they see one. It is an energy field of enormous and unbeatable strength, which issues from an alien planet or spacecraft, drawing the fearless Captain Kirk and his crew, slowly but surely, into the jaws of the waiting enemy.

At the sight of a passing piece of quiche, Yates freezes. The head is lowered and the nose rises to correct his aim. A magnetic stare is then fixed on the morsel, drawing it closer and closer until it is consumed. If the offering does not seem to move at the required speed, the beam is then transferred to the eyes of the holder. This always achieves the required result, as certainly as night follows day. Thinking of the beam of God's love, bringing strangers into his kingdom, I praise him for the loving, attracting work of the Holy Spirit. George Carey, Archbishop of Canterbury, once described the work of the Holy Spirit in these terms, when he spoke of the floodlights that brighten a building at night. One might hardly notice a building during the day. We wander past, as if it had no effect on our lives at all. But at night the building is lit up, seen for miles around. It attracts our eye and our wonder. As the beam lights up the building, so the Holy Spirit points us to Jesus, showing us the truth. Despite all our faltering attempts at evangelism, despite all our efforts in mission, it is he and he alone who does the business in the end. Many of us seem to have avoided the pull of God quite successfully for a number of years but, eventually, we have to come to him. When we do, the experience is far from fearful: it is pure delight.

Having washed the car one sunny Saturday afternoon, my wife asked me to collect up the hose pipe. This entailed following the pipe, hand over hand, to where it went over the garden gate. Off I went down the path, while Yates sat by the gate, wondering what joys might be in store. Opening the gate and stepping boldly through it, I felt the cold shock of dirty water, as my foot landed in the bucket. Then the other one! Yates positively gurgled with pleasure. 'Don't kick the bucket, Dad!' He followed my squelching footsteps back down the path, and sat smirking while I dragged off the wet socks and threw them down. Then, from a few feet away, there it was again. The Tractor Beam was switched on. Down went the black head, up came the nose, and my dirty wet socks were subjected to the full force. Nothing else in the world existed for him at that point, just the socks. How dearly he longed to possess them!

19

Pigeons and Pizzas

Then those who feared the LORD talked with each other, and the LORD listened and heard.

Malachi 3:16

Yates honestly tries to be obedient to his training—he really does! It would be a very dangerous thing for me if he continued to follow his natural instincts, rushing off to be friendly with other animals, or chasing them out of sight. Within limits this sort of fellowship is fine, but once in harness it has to be absolutely forbidden. In this regard he has tremendous self-control—usually. I do not remember being warned about this on my initial training course in Leamington Spa, but the first time he chose to exercise his own freewill was frightening! It was in Stratford that I first suspected him. Walking across an open square, instructor in attendance, he suddenly veered away to the right and picked up speed. Panic set in. Where were we going now? He was getting too excited; had he remembered he was supposed to be looking after me?

A few more steps, and I was right in amongst it: a great crowd of scuttling, flapping pigeons began to take off all around me. This was terrifying for me, but what fun for a dog! Labradors are used as gun dogs. Could this be some other distant echo of a hunting skill—putting up the birds? I was so wrong! Yates had no interest in the pigeons whatsoever. That part of his training, at least, had held firm. His interest was, it turned out, the same as theirs. His eyes were set on something far more interesting. In the middle of the square was a park bench. On it, in the afternoon sunshine, happily unaware of the chaos they were causing, sat two old ladies engrossed in sharing a cold pizza with any pigeon that would come near enough. Pizzas are extremely desirable to guide dogs. Their acute sense of smell seems to be able to pick up the scent from a tremendous range. The first I knew of this was that Yates sat down at the ladies' feet, head lifted up towards them to display an attitude of agonizing hunger. Before I could ask any passer-by where I had got to, one of the ladies said, "Isn't he sweet! He looks so hungry." Her friend asked me, "Can we give him a piece?"

I managed to disentangle Yates from his new pensioner friends and we went on our way, with him mumbling something under his breath about the need to feed the hungry in this world.

Since those early days, Yates' self-control when meeting other animals has been exceptional. We have walked past stray dogs, without a twitch. We have sauntered alongside parked cars in which mongrels were yapping and jumping, with only a disapproving shake of the black head. We have strolled through many a town square covered in pigeons without batting an eyelid. There is, however, one animal that he finds quite irresistible: another guide dog. The first sign that there is another one in the vicinity appears while we are still some way off. Yates' tail comes right up into the back of the hand that holds the harness. That's my signal to get ready; nothing else will cause it to rise that far when he is doing serious work. Then, a few feet away, he turns aside from his chosen route, the tail picks up speed to a dramatic level, and we take the last three steps at the run! All I have to do now is say, "Hello, there's another guide dog!" The greeting is always reciprocated.

Guide dogs have something special between them, I have no

doubt. Having met, the two of them will stand, nose to nose, swapping funny stories about their owners, for as long as they are allowed to. They are, I am sure, true gossips! In the meantime, the conversation between the two guide dog owners is usually of a similar nature. We, too, exchange stories about life with a dog, stories that are always full of trust and love and joy. These encounters are a great delight. Each time we say goodbye, every time we leave another guide dog/owner team, the same yearning begins to envelop me; the same question rises up from the meeting: why cannot we Christians gossip about Jesus like that? Why cannot we swap stories of our experiences with a living God? Should they not be far more interesting than doggy tales? The Church rightly teaches the biblical condemnation of gossiping; but how about encouraging the 'talkers' in our churches to evangelise? I suppose it does not have to be quite as dramatic as all that. The first sermon preached each Sunday is by the pastor, but it could be by us. We preach a message of good cheer when we say "Good morning" to those we meet as we are parking the car or walking to the church door. We preach a message of welcome when we slide over in the pew instead of forcing others to squeeze past us. We preach a message of hope and joy when we sing the hymns. We preach a message about the power of prayer when we let someone know that we are praying for them. We preach a message of love when we smile and say hello to a visitor. We preach a message about the importance of the Scriptures when we listen carefully to the Bible being read. We preach a message of faith when we share a prayer request with another Christian. We preach a message of encouragement when we voice praise to the Lord. So many messages can be preached, in other ways, *before* the pastor stands up to give the sermon. If our message is positive, faithful and consistent, then the message from the pulpit will be so much more effective!

20

Find the Way

I gain understanding from your precepts; therefore I hate every wrong path. Your word is a lamp to my feet and a light for my path.

Psalm 119:104–5

It was high summer in Lincolnshire. We had gone to spend a few days with my mother-in-law and, having assured ourselves that all was well with her, we made ready for the four hour trip home to Wales. One problem remained unresolved. Our hostess had been invited to a wedding and, as ladies always seem to remark on these occasions, she had nothing to wear. In a last minute rush, we visited the local department store; there, after much going back and forth, we found just the right thing. However, the right size was not in stock. One quick phone call set us on the right road. They found one for us in their Lincoln branch and, happily, that city was right on our path home. So to Lincoln we went. Our usual track home took us down the city's by-pass, and so this was to be our first real sortie into the centre of town. Leaving the main road, Ginnie followed the signs to the car park. Yates glued his nose to the back window of the car, watching out for the clothing store we needed to find. We succeeded in locating a multi-storey car park on the outskirts of town, but Yates failed to see the store or, if he did, he said nothing. Leaving the car, the three of us set off in search of the shop. A kind lady gave good directions: "You go down here about a quarter of a mile. Then turn left over the river and cross the main road."

Yates put one foot forward, but then had to stop. There were more instructions to come. She went on, "After that, turn right and go on for about another quarter of a mile, and turn left into the shopping centre. The shop you're looking for is up there on the right through a small gap in the houses. Just cross over the pelican crossing, and...." Our minds began to blur.

Asking a few more times, we eventually found it. Around the store we walked, in ever-decreasing circles, until the garment had been chosen and paid for. Now we needed the post office, to send the clothes to Ginnie's mother in time for the wedding.

"Can you tell us how to find the post office?" Ginnie asked. Out of the shop we went, turning right as instructed and up the hill. Left, right, then around the corner, and left again. There it was. Having successfully completed our business in the post office, we walked back out into the sunshine and wondered.

"How's your sense of direction?" Ginnie asked me. "We have to get back to the car, somehow!" I had to admit I was totally lost. I guessed that Yates was probably beyond confusion, if not dizzy. We had gone this way and that, around and around, and had absolutely no idea in which direction to set off. We were, indeed, lost. Had we been clever and taken note of the name of the car park, or even the street it was in, we might have had some hope—but we had not. I felt very vulnerable and I had no answers. "Do you think Yates knows the way?" Ginnie was scraping the bottom of the barrel for ideas, now.

'Well,' I thought, 'we could try the 'Find the Way' command and let him lead.' After all, I reasoned, that is the way that God would like us to work for him. He wants us to be vulnerable—not to the world, but to him. There was nothing else to do in our 'lostness' but become trusting followers. Similarly, every

Christian has to reach the point of realising that we are first and foremost disciples of our Lord Jesus Christ, walking by trust and faith. Our discipleship can only properly be maintained throughout our lives through our prayer, worship and the study of Scripture, the driving force being the need to deepen our individual relationship with God. Creating that desire in us is the work of the Holy Spirit. The Christian continues his or her own walk through life, but in a particular way, the path God has given us. We need to find the way. This way of God often seems to be a way of weakness and vulnerability, rather akin to where we were with Yates at that moment.

One great part of the news of the Gospel is that God became human and vulnerable, choosing that way to reveal himself among his people. Jesus did not cling to his divine power, but became like us ordinary folk in every way except sin. He brought new life to others, and his vulnerability was an essential part of his revelation of the love of God. There is one state which all Christians share, and it is this: at our Christian re-birth, however each individual may define it, the divine Lord comes to put a new Spirit within us. His will is that our souls will then become vehicles for the display of his divine splendour. To allow this divine purpose to be realised, we have to be trusting and vulnerable, available to him in our inner places. God is not always glorified in what we do, but in what we can be. What we are is the fallout of our worship rather than our activities. Central to the Christian faith is: 'My life for yours'. If we interpret this basic principle in ways which lead to total availability to those we spend time with, then we entirely miss the mechanism through which God really works in his love. Loving others fruitfully, and loving God, are not two separate issues. Fruitful and healing love for others only grows as our relationship with God deepens. The depth of this relationship is entirely dependent on how much we are prepared to give up to him. It is a question of whether we are willing to be open enough to allow ourselves to receive, both directly from God and through others. At times this can certainly seem like being vulnerable, though his love is such that we need have no fear. The constant temptation is to go on giving at any physical or emotional cost, believing that this is what Christ wants from us. Our natural instinct is to try to solve everybody's problems for them, and we become frustrated when we do not know how to do so. Our task is to help people both to bring their problems to God in prayer and to apply his Word to those difficulties.

There is something much more important than 'Christian work'. We Christians need to know the peace and acceptance of being in a secure place of intimacy with God, holding our own darkness to his light, before we are ever truly able to encourage others to go that way. The Christian who has travelled deeply into his or her own heart, and found that intimate place of meeting with Jesus, discovers with surprise two things about it. First, it is like a womb: a place of peace and security. Second, it is a place from which God reaches out, offering to embrace everyone we meet, at their point of need, surrounding them with love. We begin to see that from this place of God's love which we have found in our innermost being, that divine love, or 'living water' flows out to others. We begin to discover what Jesus meant, when he said that 'the Kingdom of God is within you'.[1]

I have used the trust I need to place in my guide dog as a 'picture' to point towards the deepest issue for us all. Can we really trust God? We can extend the metaphor a little further. Trusting Yates puts me in a place of extreme vulnerability, not towards others around me, or even lamp posts and public benches, but to him. I am not vulnerable to ice cream signs, open car doors and passing people now that I have Yates. I am vulnerable to him. Does that trust and vulnerability pay off? We tried it outside the post office in Lincoln city centre. "Come on then, Yates. Find the way!" He turned his head as if to say, "Absolutely no problem, Dad!" Off he set, an assured spring in his step. Where were we going now? There was nothing to do but follow. We had no idea where the car park was, but Yates had a certainty about him that shouted 'leadership'. We turned left, and we turned right. Down that street we went, and across that road, all the while just following our leader. Yates marched on. He found the road crossings and the traffic lights. He trotted

[1]Luke 17:21

on around this corner, and ignored that turning. On and on we went. Suddenly, he lunged to my left, and I yanked him back. This is a normal reaction to sudden doggy movements, as they usually signify the presence of a discarded beefburger! "Leave it!" I growled. He stopped and looked up at me, confused by my lack of appreciation.

"That's the entrance to the car park!" Ginnie exclaimed.

Afterword

*He who sacrifices thank offerings honours me, and he prepares
the way so that I may show him the salvation of God.*

Psalm 50:23

One thought summarises my first three years with Yates and
fills me with peace: that our Father, together with the Son and
the Holy Spirit, are carefully leading me through this life and
then home to him.

*Thank you, Lord, for bringing Yates into my life. Thank you for
all that I have learned about you through being with him.*

*Thank you for showing me your faithfulness, your steadfast
love and your longing to be trusted.*

*Thank you that I know to walk through this life with you, and
that, when my travelling is done, you will bring me safely home.*

Amen.

Also from Terra Nova Publications:

Books

HEALING AT THE WELL
Mike Endicott — ISBN 1901949079 — £7.99

THE HOT LINE
Peter Lawrence — ISBN 0952268868 — £5.99

DOING WHAT COMES SUPERNATURALLY
Peter Lawrence — ISBN 0952268841 — £5.99

CHRISTIAN HEALING
Peter Lawrence — ISBN 0952268876 — £3.95

GROWING IN THE WORD
Hilary Latham — ISBN 1901949028 — £5.99

A FAITH THAT WORKS
Don Latham — ISBN 1901949001 — £6.99

THE STRUGGLE
Hartmut Kopsch — ISBN 190194901X — £7.99

FROM FREEMASONRY TO FREEDOM
Stanley Trickett — ISBN 1901949052 — £4.50

SERVANTS OF THE LIVING GOD
Lawrence, Woolmer & others — ISBN 1901949044 — £5.99

GOD AND THE TROUBLES OF LIFE
Paul Griffiths — ISBN 1901949095 — £6.99

Booklets

BEING UNMISTAKABLY CHRISTIAN AT WORK
Don Latham — ISBN 1901949060 — £3.50

STAIRWAY TO HEAVEN
Peter Lawrence — ISBN 1901949036 — 99p

Study Resources

TOWARDS CHRISTIAN MATURITY
Hilary Latham — ISBN 0953149412 — £6.95